T0348054

FILM STARS

Stars are an integral part of every major film industry in the world. In this pivotal new series, each book is devoted to an international movie star, looking at the development of their identity, their acting and performance methods, the cultural significance of their work, and their influence and legacy. Taking a wide range of different stars, including George Clooney, Brigitte Bardot and Dirk Bogarde among others, this series encompasses the sphere of silent and sound acting, Hollywood and non-Hollywood areas of cinema, and child and adult forms of stardom. With its broad range, but a focus throughout on the national and historical dimensions to film, the series offers students and researchers a new approach to studying film.

SERIES EDITORS
Martin Shingler and Susan Smith

PUBLISHED TITLES
Barbara Stanwyck *Andrew Klevan*
Brigitte Bardot *Ginette Vincendeau*
Carmen Miranda *Lisa Shaw*
Elizabeth Taylor *Susan Smith*
Mickey Rourke *Keri Walsh*
Nicole Kidman *Pam Cook*
Penélope Cruz *Ann Davies*
Star Studies: A Critical Guide *Martin Shingler*

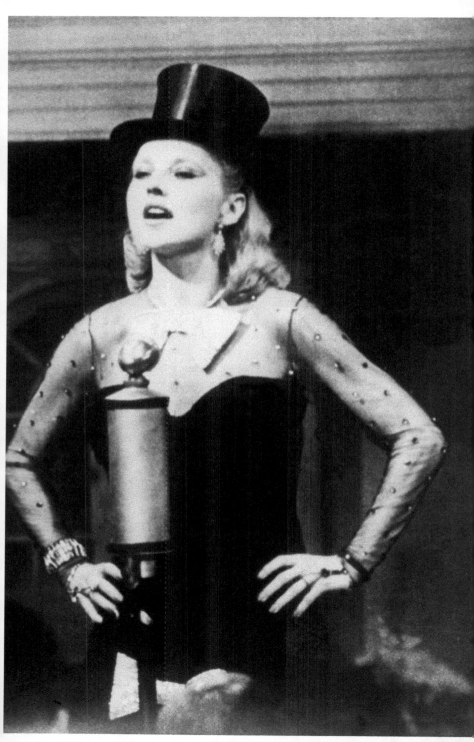

Hanna SCHYGULLA

ULRIKE SIEGLOHR

palgrave
macmillan

A BFI book published by Palgrave Macmillan

To Jim

First published in 2014 by
PALGRAVE MACMILLAN

on behalf of the

BRITISH FILM INSTITUTE
21 Stephen Street, London W1T 1LN
www.bfi.org.uk

There's more to discover about film and television through the BFI. Our world-renowned archive, cinemas, festivals, films, publications and learning resources are here to inspire you.

Designed by couch
Cover images: (front) *Rio das Mortes* (Rainer Werner Fassbinder, 1970), Janus Film und Fernsehen/antiteater-X-Film; (back) *Faust* (Aleksandr Sukurov, 2011), © Proline-film/ © Filmförderung Russia

Set by Cambrian Typesetters, Camberley, Surrey

British Library Cataloguing-in-Publication Data
A catalogue record for this book is available from the British Library
A catalog record for this book is available from the Library of Congress

ISBN   978-1-84457-463-6 (pb)
eISBN 978-1-83871-606-6
ePDF 978-1-84457-828-3

(*previous page*) Homage to Dietrich in *Lili Marleen* (1981)

CONTENTS

ACKNOWLEDGMENTS

Thanks to Moritz Mescher at the Videothek Filmgallery 451 in Berlin, who was always kind and most helpful in tracking down rare videos. I also would like to thank the friendly staff at the Bibliothek der Deutschen Kinemathek, Berlin. Special thanks go to Sophia Contento and to Philippa Hudson for their gracious and unflappable efficiency in organising the publishing side of the project.

I'm most grateful to friends: Martin Brady, Frédérique Delacoste, Christine Gledhill, Peter Hames, Sarah and Mel Hill, Ilse and Martin Jesinghausen, Wiltrud Niehl, Ginette Vincendeau and my sister, Christel Sieglohr, all of whom have been generously supportive of my research by sending me press cuttings, lending me old videos, providing me both with specific references and broader advice, and generally sharing their impressions of Hanna Schygulla's work.

I owe boundless gratitude to my friend Martin Shingler not only for suggesting this book, but also for being available throughout for lively discussions, for incisive reading, and for generous editorial support – all well beyond the call of duty and friendship.

My partner, Jim Cook, bore the brunt of the inevitable tensions I experienced researching and writing the book. He was unfailingly supportive, helping me to clarify ideas even at times against my initial resistance.

INTRODUCTION

Blonde with shortish tousled curls, dark-rimmed eyes and pale lipstick, wearing a diaphanous blouse and the shortest of miniskirts, unzipping her high boots, she reveals her black suspender straps and the bare strip of flesh between knickers and nylon stockings.

With this tantalising shot, Rainer Werner Fassbinder introduced his star, Hanna Schygulla, in *Liebe ist kälter als der Tod/Love Is Colder than Death* (1969). A few films later, in the opening shot of *Rio das Mortes* (1971), she is presented standing in sexy black underwear, bra, suspender belt, stockings and high heels, twiddling her curls. Thereafter, a flash of Schygulla's naked thighs is filmed not only by Fassbinder, as her inimitable lethargic erotic posturing also becomes the iconic image for many other directors: most notably, Marco Ferreri and Andrzej Wajda. At the height of her stardom in the early 1980s, American critics especially – enraptured by her non-Hollywood sex appeal – compared her to Marlene Dietrich, *the* original German star, who had also started her career by exposing her suspender-belted thighs in *The Blue Angel* (1930).

However, erotic allure did not distinguish Schygulla from any number of young actresses in European and Hollywood cinema, nor did her suspenders enable her to evolve from Fassbinder's iconic anti-star into a glamorous international and transnational star.[1] What made this possible was her formative training as a performer in both experimental theatre and artisanal/low-budget New German

Cinema. Schygulla started out in 1967 as an actor in Fassbinder's anti-authoritarian theatre group, the Action-Theater, a collective that embraced the radical ideas of Bertolt Brecht and the libertarian ideals of the contemporary North American The Living Theatre.[2] Ever since, Schygulla's career has been consistently evaluated through the prism of Fassbinder, where she is acclaimed as his muse and enigmatic star. In this context, her work with other equally prominent auteurs is typically seen as less remarkable.

When I embarked on this book, I was particularly intrigued by the German critical consensus that, after her collaboration with Fassbinder, Schygulla never again managed to maintain a compelling star persona. Indeed, the reasons for this consensus became one of the key issues to be explored in my study through close textual analyses, as well as by comparing divergent national receptions.[3] Nevertheless, I should acknowledge that even my own first sight of Schygulla on screen (in *Katzelmacher* during its release in Germany in 1969) came about due to my interest in the cinema of Fassbinder. Though I was fascinated by this and many of the more stylised early Fassbinder films, Schygulla herself made very little impression on me and I remained unimpressed by her languid movements, her Bavarian intonation and her indolent blonde sexiness. Later, in the 1990s, as a German expatriate in Britain and a PhD student, my academic interest in this national cinema was inspired by Thomas Elsaesser's seminal book *New German Cinema*.[4] Consequently, in 2011, when I began work on this book for the BFI *Film Stars* series, my initial point of departure was my long-held interest in Fassbinder and the New German Cinema. However, as research for the book progressed, I came to appreciate Schygulla's untiring readiness to take risks, to experiment and to change, and I experienced many unexpected revelations, particularly while watching the actress performing in films by directors other than Fassbinder. Above all, I increasingly admired Schygulla's intelligence in managing her performance skills, particularly a capacity to turn what critics have perceived as her manneristic limitation to her own advantage. Consequently, my study bears witness to Schygulla's increasing versatility and the fact that her work with a wide range of distinguished international directors has afforded the actor greater agency, as well as producing a more naturalistic acting style. With her increasing versatility, Schygulla has consistently proved those critics wrong who perceived her as lacking in talent, while defying the oft-repeated predictions that her career would end with Fassbinder's death.

Though Schygulla may not have become a Hollywood star, she certainly did acquire transnational stardom through her work with a range of international directors in different national cinemas and languages. This, I will argue, is a testament to her resourcefulness and talent. So while her collaboration with Fassbinder made her a national star and raised her international profile, I shall also argue that Schygulla was largely responsible for turning herself into a transnational star. It is this career trajectory that will be examined in more detail in the following chapters.

This book is structured chronologically, each chapter focusing on a particular career stage, with detailed examination of key films and their international reception. With over ninety films to choose from (see Filmography), I have concentrated on those that best indicate the range of her performance style, selecting films that made the most significant contribution to the evolution of her star persona. I do, however, include some lesser-known films here that help to demonstrate the full extent of her performance skills. Chapter 1, which covers her first distinct phase with Fassbinder, examines the formative years of Schygulla's rise to national fame through the films she made with him, ending with their acrimonious break-up. This experimental period – when alternative types of creative environment were being explored – along with its broader historical-cultural determinants, is fundamental to Schygulla's significance in Fassbinder's developing oeuvre. This phase is also vital for understanding how her very specific and idiosyncratic early training constructed an (anti-)star image, which subsequently remained at the core of her international star persona. The main films under discussion here include *Love Is Colder than Death*, *Whity* (1971) and *Fontane Effi Briest/Effi Briest* (1974). Chapter 2 briefly discusses the period when she became a 'jobbing' actor, appearing in such films as Wim Wenders's *Falsche Bewegung/Wrong Move* (1975), before returning to Fassbinder and achieving her international breakthrough with *Die Ehe der Maria Braun/The Marriage of Maria Braun* (1979) and *Lili Marleen* (1981). With *Maria Braun*, she became the star whose persona for a time eclipsed Fassbinder, certainly for the New York critics, leading to a further estrangement and their final separation.

Chapter 3 charts how, having finally separated from Fassbinder, Schygulla went on to work with some eminent European auteurs (e.g. Jean-Luc Godard, Carlos Saura, Ettore Scola, Andrzej Wajda and Marco Ferreri) alongside other commercial international film and television directors. It also explores why, despite Hollywood beckoning, the roles did not materialise. However, the main focus of this chapter is the divergent, nationally specific reception of her performances in Ferreri's *Storia di Piera/The Story of Piera* (1983) and in Wajda's *Eine Liebe in Deutschland/A Love in Germany* (1983). While Schygulla garnered eulogies in some countries, the negative West German reception of these films marked the nadir of her domestic career, yet makes for a fascinating case study for transnational stardom. Chapter 4 describes how the actress shrewdly negotiated the process of ageing through diversification, reinventing herself, for instance, as an internationally acclaimed cabaret chanteuse when the film offers dried up. However, the chapter also examines how during this period she established an important working relationship with the radical political Israeli film-maker Amos Gitai, as well as working with a new generation of German directors. It focuses in particular on her highly praised comeback in

Fatih Akin's *Auf der anderen Seite/The Edge of Heaven* (2007), from which she emerged as a formidably intelligent actor rather than a glamorous fading star. Consequently, this film provides the main focus of the final chapter, demonstrating beyond doubt that the scope of Schygulla's acting ability was never limited to the idiosyncratic mannerism of her work with Fassbinder. Despite this, the aim of this study is not to undermine the significance of Hanna Schygulla's working relationship with Fassbinder but rather to pay more attention to her agency as both actor and performer in constructing and reconstructing her career. This is to better understand how her determination to work with other directors has developed her performance skills and enabled her to achieve transnational stardom.

1 FASSBINDER'S MUSE AND ANTI-STAR, 1967–74

As Fassbinder's seductive and enigmatic anti-star, Schygulla captivated German critics and audiences with an early screen image of corrupted naivety. This nascent persona – at times innocent siren (e.g. *Katzelmacher*), at other times debased proletarian vamp (e.g. *Love Is Colder than Death, Götter der Pest/Gods of the Plague* [1970] and *Whity*) – manifests itself in characters ranging from prostitutes to nightclub singers and servants; all figures with petit-bourgeois aspirations who dream of escape and happiness until disillusionment leads to betrayal and revenge. Before international critics would acclaim her as the 'New Marlene' in the 1980s, German critics perceived her more like a home-grown Marilyn Monroe pastiche – a '*Vorstadt* Marilyn/backstreet Marilyn'[1] whose streetwise femininity was associated with the working-class tenement blocks and dank courtyards of districts situated just outside the city centre.[2] Schygulla's evocative image not only appealed to critics and film historians but, with its overall tone of disillusionment, powerfully resonated with the failed utopianism experienced by the post-1968 generation.

Given the success of this persona, a key issue for consideration is whether Fassbinder was the flamboyant Svengali 'author' of it all. Was Schygulla merely one of his puppets or, alternatively, was she his muse and inspiration, guiding him on? Most reviewers and academics have, at least implicitly, located their assessment of her somewhere along this spectrum, considering Schygulla's career through the dominant Fassbinder prism. As this chapter will demonstrate, the actress was indeed at times a willing puppet on Fassbinder's strings, perceiving that such a role could be advantageous to her career. At other times, however, she maintained her independence and agency by working with a number of different German directors, extending her acting range and expanding her career prospects. I will argue that this was a mutually beneficial professional relationship from the outset, with Schygulla actively shaping her emerging star persona while Fassbinder simultaneously developed his auteurist style and vision.[3]

A scene in *Rio das Mortes* captures some of the complexity of their relationship. Here, Hanna (Schygulla) is seen in a bar dancing in a clinch with a stranger (Fassbinder) to a very slow blues number. Then, when the music changes to Elvis Presley's upbeat 'Jailhouse Rock', they dance separately, with Fassbinder merely standing upright, nodding his head and clapping stiffly, while admiring Hanna's solo dancing. Schygulla's whole body gyrates, her hands and arms waving wildly in the air, her face animated by a series of continuously changing expressions, her eyes half-closed and lips wide open, mouthing and pouting. By breaking free and expressing her personality rather than the character's, the actress revealed a side to her that Fassbinder admired but which was at some distance from his own conception of her screen persona. Twenty-five years later, Schygulla would recall this scene as 'a moment of total liberation!'[4] Thus, her dancing and laughter illustrate that while lascivious somnambulism was the most pervasive aspect of her acting style in Fassbinder's films, there also existed an undercurrent of disruptive vivacity that could not be accommodated in their work together. The scene anticipates the inevitable rift between Schygulla and Fassbinder. While the Fassbinder roles may have constructed a coherent screen persona for Schygulla the star, they failed to offer Schygulla the actor the means of self-realisation that she increasingly craved (as will be discussed below).

The formative period with Fassbinder: experimental theatre and New German Cinema

Born in 1943 in Kattowitz in German-occupied Poland, and daughter of a timber merchant, Schygulla fled with her mother in 1945 to Munich. Her father, a prisoner of war (POW), only joined them in 1948. Subsequently, she went to grammar school, spent a year as an au pair in Paris and then, with the aim of becoming a teacher, studied German and Romance languages at Munich University.[5] Around 1966, while still studying languages, she started taking lessons at the professional Fridl-Leonard acting school, where she encountered Fassbinder. However, apart from rehearsing some scenes together, both recalled that they had little contact and seem not even to have liked each other. Schygulla soon got bored, lost faith in her acting ability and left after a few months, apparently without too much regret. However, Fassbinder also (and contradictorily) claimed later that it was there and then that he had identified her as his future star: 'As if I'd been struck by lightning [it became crystal clear] that Hanna Schygulla would one day be the star of my films, ... she would be an essential cornerstone possibly, maybe even something like their driving force.'[6]

Schygulla returned to acting in autumn 1967 when Fassbinder tracked her down, offering her a last-minute replacement leading role in Sophocles's *Antigone*, directed by Peer Raben and probably inspired by The Living Theatre's performance of the same play.[7] Although she only had a couple of days to rehearse before playing her part to the acclaim of the audience and critics, Fassbinder remembered her first public stage performance as an outstanding achievement, 'magnificent, of extraordinary pathos and intensity',[8] and it was acknowledged as such somewhat begrudgingly by the collective. Subsequently playing key roles for the Action-Theater and the renamed anti-teater,[9] her training as an actor was on the job. She recalls that critics liked her performances, perceiving her as 'a mixture of artifice and naivety, both somnambulistic and dilettantish'[10] – terms which later came to describe her performance style.

Schygulla continued to work with Fassbinder as he moved into low-budget film-making in the late 1960s while still directing radical political theatre. Off stage or off screen, she was pretty rather than strikingly beautiful: of average height, slim but with solid thighs and small breasts, she had big blue eyes, high cheekbones, a broad forehead in an expansive face with a longish pointed nose, wide, full, sensual lips, small, even teeth and a strong chin. A mass of curly blonde hair softened her features to resemble her teenage screen idols Brigitte Bardot and Marilyn Monroe. On screen, careful shading would sculpt her bone structure to break up the fleshy expansiveness of her pronounced Slavic features, while lighting, along with make-up, was key in enhancing her round facial contours, focusing on the eyes and lips while masking the dominance of her nose. 'Curly hair and kohl rimmed eyes, something between a doll and silent film diva of the Munich backstreets'[11] is Schygulla's own description of her image at this time.

To understand the forces shaping Schygulla's image, it is important to place her theatre and film work with Fassbinder within a broader political and cultural context. The late 1960s in West Germany was a time of counter-cultural activities, student rebellion and general political upheaval. In this context, specific cinematic state cultural policies resulted in financial assistance, giving radical left-wingers and inexperienced film-makers the opportunity to make films. The New German Cinema,[12] as the movement became known, first developed domestically in the 1960s, but by the mid-1970s, auteurs such as Fassbinder, Werner Herzog and Wim Wenders were gaining international prominence. Conceived as a national cinema and underpinned by a cultural notion of film-making, New German Cinema distanced itself from the market values of both Hollywood and contemporary mainstream German cinema. In West Germany, the New German Cinema found favour primarily with radicalised students, producing a select but devoted audience.

Fassbinder's *Love Is Colder than Death*, which starred Schygulla (see below for more detailed analysis), was one of the first feature films released by this new generation of film-makers, and, indeed, the aesthetically eclectic and politically radical New German Cinema's body of work is unthinkable without Fassbinder. This is partly because of the highly idiosyncratic stamp he brought to his films and partly because the New German Cinema – also known in German as *Autorenkino*[13] – like that of its predecessor the French New Wave, privileged its directors.[14] Thus, Fassbinder, as director and creator of meaning, became *the* star and a marketing brand name from the start, with Schygulla increasingly regarded in early film reviews as his muse and non-commercial (anti-)star. In the words of one critic, the director was its 'heart, the beating, vibrant centre of [it] all'.[15] However, to extend the metaphor, without Schygulla as his leading star, Fassbinder's oeuvre would have lacked the life-blood vital to this heart.

Fassbinder's status as the iconic star director of the New German Cinema impacted directly upon Schygulla's developing star persona. With his flamboyant and uncompromising identity (political and sexual), Fassbinder quickly became the focus of media attention rather than his much more reticent star. His confrontational manner with journalists and his excessive lifestyle of drugs, alcohol and upfront promiscuity (gay *and* bisexual) were easy fodder for the tabloid press, as they were at times for the broadsheets, being frequently noted in press coverage of his films. Fassbinder quickly acquired an iconic image, with his recognisable features (round face, high cheekbones, slanted eyes, prominent nose and full lips) and his regular attire of battered leather jacket, trilby hat and tight trousers.

In addition to this distinctive image and self-conscious '*enfant terrible*' persona, he also made frequently Hitchcock-like cameo appearances in his films, even starring in a number of them. Most of all, since his early films were known to be autobiographical in a '*roman-à-clef*' sense, he knowingly exploited his private life for publicity and promotional material. Given the combination of Fassbinder's media ubiquity and Schygulla's intense desire for privacy during this period, it would have been near impossible for the actress to develop an equally striking star persona. Interestingly, when she finally did overshadow him, he took revenge (see Chapter 2).

Alongside a commercial West German star system, from the 1970s on, the government-subsidised New German Cinema developed its own star system as something distinct from the earlier generation of film-makers, such as the members of the 1960s Young German Cinema, who had tended to use lay actors.[16] Although actors often remained closely associated with one particular director,[17] they also contributed to a pool of performers who were easily recognisable across the body of New German Cinema. An individual actor would bring their previously accrued persona (achieved through the kind of roles they had played for one director) to their parts in other films by different directors.[18] Stars like Schygulla, who acted in New German films directed by several directors, were part of a group of highly visible actors who were pivotal in providing coherence across New German Cinema and contributed to its later international success.[19]

Fassbinder, as both a maverick and autodidact, had gathered around him a devoted entourage, a 'pocket version of the star system'[20] reminiscent of Warhol's Factory of underground super-stars. The regular appearance of the same leading and supporting actors across his productions became a defining hallmark of his oeuvre, a stability that helped him to be so productive. This point is well made by Thomas Elsaesser, who states that Fassbinder's work is unified thanks to a stable infrastructure consisting of technical and production collaborators, 'the equivalent of a mini-studio system'[21]

Fassbinder with his anti-star and the collective

(including specialists in sets, costume, camera, music, editing), along with the 'extended family' of performers (including ex-members of the radical theatre group) and the regular cast/supporting actors, comprised of theatre-trained actors or stars of the West German commercial cinema. In this context, Schygulla (his foremost star) coexisted with Margit Carstensen, Elisabeth Trissenaar and Barbara Sukowa, although none of these would quite belong to Fassbinder's inner circle.[22]

Even though Schygulla was a member of the 1968 re-formed anti-teater collective, privately she kept her distance. The collective made themselves available for any role or technical function, whereas Schygulla remained a 'guest-star', one who, according to Fassbinder, demanded the right to participate 'only if a particular role and production concept were of sufficient interest to her'.[23] Fassbinder complained that political commitment was less important to Schygulla 'than one's personal brilliance in a role',[24] and that she was 'conspicuously terrible in minor roles that don't interest her'.[25] While Schygulla's privileged status was often resented by her colleagues, the actress was able to make the transition from non-commercial anti-star to acclaimed international star by being simultaneously central and remote.[26]

Acting with Fassbinder: rehearsal techniques and influences

Especially from the late 1960s through to the mid-1970s, most of Fassbinder's associates recall how much fun it was to work with him,[27] despite his unsettling sadomasochistic psycho-games – inviting closeness (even sexual intimacy for some) only then to reject them. During this period, the private and public sphere were intertwined as sites of contestation for many (as in the feminist slogan of the time, 'the personal is political'), but few directors explored this aspect of the zeitgeist as explicitly and as consistently as Fassbinder, whose intimate knowledge of his regular actors was exploited to trigger particular kinds of performance. As Schygulla commented, 'Fassbinder was like a panther and one never knew whether he would show claws or affection; in both he was a master.'[28] In fact, his approach was different with Schygulla, whom he carefully coaxed, and from whom he maintained a certain distance. As Fassbinder himself later remarked, 'Privately we rather avoided any contact. This was probably from both sides, albeit unconsciously, because we both knew we would not be able to continue working with each other if we were to be personally involved.'[29] Fassbinder directed Schygulla and his other actors usually with little rehearsal, most typically with one run-through, one rehearsal, two camera takes and no establishing shot.[30] Avoiding discussion or explanation, Fassbinder relied on his charismatic panache to set a certain tone. While he knew exactly what he wanted in terms of framing, 'he wasn't one to give you all the details of what he wanted; there was some space for you to create'.[31] His methods aimed not to deliver psychological realism, since he was more interested in creating an explicitly artificial performance style of emotional signifiers. For Schygulla, this produced a manneristic style of acting that referenced, to the point of parody, admired stars such as Marilyn Monroe, Brigitte Bardot and Marlene Dietrich.

Schygulla later recalled the audience's bemused response to the manneristic acting that formed so much a part of her anti-star persona. 'The audience could never be quite sure: is that good what she is doing, or is it terrible? Is she beautiful or ugly? Is this banal or meaningful?'[32] In the context of Fassbinder's staging of a film as if it was a theatre play, and vice versa, the artifice of the performance inevitably became foregrounded. In these early years, the role was played as a role, sometimes through over-the-top acting and non-natural gestures, at other times through 'inappropriate' under-expressivity. Consequently, the actors embodied the role without producing the sense of a psychologically fleshed-out character. This gap between role and performance (which produces the distancing effect) undermined a believable diegesis and was created in part through an acting style indebted to Brecht's Epic Theatre.[33] However, Brecht was not the only influence on Fassbinder's approach to working with actors. Jean-Marie Straub, a critically acclaimed and politically radical film director, also made a deep impact on Fassbinder during the late 1960s. Straub's austere, minimalist film aesthetics (again influenced by Brecht) were matched by an explicitly dilettantish and minimalist performance style. This provided Fassbinder with a prototype for a kind of anti-acting style that lent itself to the deconstruction of the petit-bourgeois values expressed by the protagonists of his early films. Meanwhile, another significant model for Fassbinder (and the New German Cinema more generally) was provided by the French New Wave, which had distanced itself from the literary tradition of Quality Cinema by adopting non-actorly performances that were noticeably more casual and less rehearsed.[34] This apparent dilettantism suited Fassbinder's pragmatism, allowing him to cast a wide range of his entourage very effectively, including those with very little acting ability.

In a general discussion about acting styles, Andrew Klevan suggests that the credibility of a performance has less to do with verisimilitude and more to do with its 'coherence and harmony with the film's environment': that is, in relation to movement, gesture, framing, composition, lighting, costume and editing.[35] Certainly Schygulla's inimitable stylisation was an outcome of Fassbinder's authorial anti-naturalistic conception of dramaturgy and, during this early period, she embodied his style better than any other actress. As subsequent chapters will demonstrate, while this overall aesthetic influence receded with time, key aspects of it nonetheless remained at the core of what became her signature style.

Schygulla: the performer as lascivious somnambulist

From 1968 until 1974, Fassbinder directed Schygulla in sixteen films across diverse genres, including one controversial soap opera television series, *Acht Stunden sind keinTag/Eight Hours Are not a Day* (1972), and many stage productions (some of them filmed), encompassing his auteurist take on gangster films, melodramas, historical costume dramas and literary adaptations, as well as the sentimental, rural, German-specific *Heimat* films. Among her many memorable roles are the pertly sexy Marie in the radically stylised and theatrical *Katzelmacher*;[36] a nightclub singer (the archetypical 'backstreet Marilyn') in the melancholic gangster film *Gods of the Plague*; or the scheming lesbian lover in *Die bitteren Tränen der Petra von Kant/The Bitter Tears of Petra von Kant* (1972).
Especially interesting for its self-conscious reflection on Schygulla's growing star image is *Warnung vor einer heiligen Nutte/Beware of a Holy Whore* (1971), which restages the chaotic production and disintegrating group dynamics of the anti-teater during the shoot of

Stylised acting with Hans Hirschmüller in
Katzelmacher (1969)

Whity.[37] Drawing on Schygulla's much-documented aloofness from
the collective, the film also sets her apart from the rest as the
glamorous star. In one sly depiction we see her dancing, self-
absorbed and narcissistically twirling only around herself.

Schygulla performed with Fassbinder in three productions by
other directors, such as her brief screen debut in Jean-Marie Straub's
*Der Bräutigam, die Komödiantin und der Zuhälter/The Bridegroom, the
Comedienne and the Pimp* (1968). However, to further her career and
expand her performance style towards naturalism, she independently
also accepted six roles by other German film-makers, including
supporting roles in Peter Fleischmann's internationally acclaimed
critical *Heimat* film[38] *Jagdszenen aus Niederbayern/Hunting Scenes from
Bavaria* (1969) and in Reinhard Hauff's television film *Die*

Revolte/The Rebellion (1969). As the curly blonde love interest, she had a major role in the burlesque gangster comedy *Das Kuckucksei im Gangsternest/The Cuckoo's Egg in the Gangster Nest* (1969)[39] and, in 1971, she won the major German film prize (the Filmband in Gold) for her role as the lead actress in Hauff's television film *Mathias Kneissl* (1970).[40] While overall, this highly productive period demonstrates the absolute centrality of Fassbinder and Schygulla's much-acclaimed collaboration, it also indicates her insistent desire to go beyond Fassbinder and to strike out on her own by intermittently working with other directors. Nonetheless, given that her persona essentially developed through work with Fassbinder, it is possible to examine her performances exclusively through roles in his films.

Although the audience booed at the 1969 Berlin Film Festival premiere of *Love Is Colder than Death*, which was Schygulla's Fassbinder screen debut, the film went on to win the Filmband in Gold for ensemble acting after it enjoyed a wider release in the wake of the critically acclaimed *Katzelmacher* (which had premiered at the 1969 Mannheim International Film Festival). *Love Is Colder than Death* is a double homage to Hollywood gangster films as refracted through the sensibilities of the French New Wave: in other words, it is an imitation of an imitation. As such, the key stylistic element is a visual citation of gestures and character framing from these films. Shot on grainy and often overexposed black-and-white stock, its aesthetic marks it out as a low-budget film. The slow, de-dramatised, bleak noirish plot of betrayal, constructed around male bonding and the figure of a femme fatale, is set among petty criminals and concerns a small-time pimp, Franz (Fassbinder), who resists joining a criminal syndicate. After he is beaten up by members of the syndicate, Franz returns to living with his prostitute girlfriend, Joanna (Schygulla), until he is tracked down and befriended by the handsome Bruno (Ulli Lommel), unaware that he is an ice-cold syndicate hit man sent out to find him. Living with Joanna as a *ménage à trois*, Bruno and Franz plan a bank robbery and, after

The first 'glamour' close-up

Bruno has killed several people to incriminate Franz, Joanna betrays him to the police in a bid to eliminate Bruno and fulfil her dreams of domestic married bliss with Franz. Bruno, however, has hired a syndicate man to kill Joanna, but he is shot in the ensuing fracas by the police as Joanna and Franz make their getaway.

The black-and-white cinematography of *Love Is Colder than Death*, which consists of very long takes with a mainly static camera, is so minimalist as to force attention onto the performers' lack of facial expressivity. This, along with their slow gestures and diction, generates a pervasive sense of artifice rather than low-life realism. The performers deliberately adopt imitative posturing to quote other actors' mannerisms, *presenting* types instead of creating psychologically rounded protagonists. Most clearly, Bruno (Lommel) pays homage to Alain Delon's killer in Jean-Pierre Melville's *Le Samuraï* (1967), with his Stetson and impassive looks. Schygulla's playing of her character as a 'backstreet Marilyn', however, is not as directly generic. Her Joanna as femme fatale is no glamour girl but rather 'a downtrodden creature who sells herself in order to buy future bourgeois happiness'.[41] Even though it is Franz

Suspenders and Rainer Werner Fassbinder in
Love Is Colder than Death (1969)

and Bruno's homosocial bonding that progresses the plot, as
Fassbinder states, 'Hanna is the key to everything ... the character she
plays is totally bogged down in bourgeois values'.[42] Significantly, *Love
Is Colder than Death* illustrates that the nascent hallmarks of Schygulla's
performance style are already manifest at the beginning of her
collaboration with Fassbinder. This includes her pervasive lethargy
of movements and gestures (with occasional animated moments),
a lascivious state of undress and sudden (disruptive) laughter.

Schygulla makes her entrance about a third of the way into the
film, at one point prefiguring what would become one of the defining
poses of her star persona: namely, the unmistakable way that she
unfastens her suspender belt. In a four-minute static take, Joanna
walks into a bedsit room where Franz is sitting at the table. She half
turns towards the camera, throwing a fur-trimmed coat onto the
chair and a handbag onto the table. Dressed in the sexy manner of
the proverbial 'tart', she puts a foot onto the bed to unzip one boot
after the other, the naked flesh of her thighs emphasised by the
camera, which is positioned at crotch height. Slowly, she lowers her

head to unhook the stockings from the suspender belt as Franz asks, 'How was it?' Very carefully, she rolls down her nylons, flinging them onto the bed, before reaching into her handbag to retrieve a purse, from which she hands Franz a few notes without directly looking at him. Turning her body towards the camera, she then walks out of the frame while he counts the money, putting one note back onto the table. Here, she indicates tired resignation and subjection to her pimp through her gestures and pose, while remaining erotically provocative for the viewing audience.

In a subsequent scene, where Bruno attempts to seduce Joanna, Schygulla's explosive laughter is introduced, demonstrating her shift in performance register. Starting with Joanna's nervous clattering as she clears the table, it moves to a moment of hesitant expectation, as she yields to Franz's insinuating caresses. This is followed by a resigned physical passivity with Bruno that suddenly explodes into convulsive laughter, until she is slapped into submissiveness. The reason for Joanna's initial nervous defiance is only revealed at the end when we deduce from her reply that Franz has pressured her to have sex with Bruno. Hence, initially Joanna remains limp and unresponsive to Bruno's seductive fumbling, with only her lowered eyes blinking, while her hand briefly taps a finger against the tumbler on the floor. When he moves to kissing her face, her lips suddenly part into a smile and then her body starts shaking with a rising giggle. Throwing her head back, she bursts into a loud, gurgling, throaty laugh, before standing up to button and tuck her blouse back in. Suddenly, Franz hits her across the face and they confront each other, locking eyes with their profiles to the camera. Schygulla's lips tighten and, twisting her body away from him, she asks in a constrained voice, 'What is this for?' 'Because you laughed at Bruno,' he replies, adding 'and he is my friend.' Her voice becomes strong and emphatic on the personal pronoun, when she asks, 'And *I*?', to which Franz replies, 'You love me anyhow.' Schygulla's actorly skill here is to make minimal facial movements such as her downcast eyes meaningful, rendering the immobility of her lips and other facial

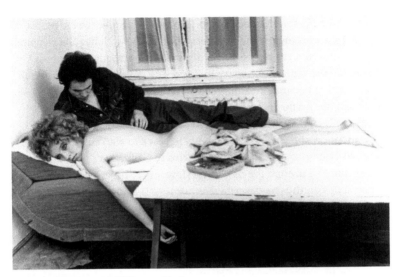

Lascivious boredom with Ulli Lommel in *Love Is Colder than Death* (1969)

muscles highly expressive. Moreover, she uses a weighed-down corporeal physicality and slowness of movement to show that her character's life is more endured than enjoyed. Through Schygulla's playing, Joanna appears to switch off her emotions as if she is not quite there, only briefly bursting into life when she laughs. Of course, Joanna's brief moment of resistance through unrestrained laughter is punished, while the male bond is reasserted.

Throughout the film, Schygulla rarely shows any animation, her face hardly registering an expression, her eyes mostly downcast. Even when the character speaks about her hopes for the future, the vocal performance is monotonous. She moves with slow resolution and, although slim, her movements convey a tired corporeal physicality, such as when she undresses with deliberate slowness by sensually wiggling out of her skirt, or lying down naked and motionless, eyes open and unfocused, next to the fully dressed lover but turned away from him.

While Franz/Fassbinder and Bruno/Lommel are active narrative agents, Joanna is merely their witness. Nevertheless, Schygulla remains the key actor here, as her performance includes reflective moments when only she is given the space to convey 'non-verbal and emotional reactions that become meaningful aspects of her interiority'.[43] Although her performance in *Love Is Colder than Death* does not yet show a fully developed signature style, idiosyncratic gestures and movement do appear to be sufficiently in place to warrant application of James Naremore's general acting terms to Schygulla's performance in this film.[44] Through the unnatural slowness of her movements, her acting style can thus be described as *ostensive* (i.e. drawing attention to itself), and this applies also to Schygulla's facial under-expressivity, which is at odds with the 'ordinary' behaviour expected in such situations. Schygulla's acting can also be considered in relation to Naremore's concepts of *representational* performance (i.e. being in character to create believable fictional protagonists) and *presentational* performance (where style draws attention to the performers as themselves, thereby overshadowing the fictional character).[45] Although these performance approaches exist on a continuum, Schygulla's acting in *Love Is Colder than Death* is strongly biased towards the presentational, with the occasional mundane quality that moves towards character revelation. There is, however, more to Schygulla's acting than her postures, gestures and expressions. Indeed, central to understanding her distinctiveness is her voice, which has been a dominant aspect of her persona and performance style.

In general the sing-song quality of Schygulla's voice has divided German critics between those who are either bewitched by its light Bavarian inflection, its mellow tone and its slow, exhaling cadences,[46] and those who find her vocal delivery mushy, 'slow and monotonous'.[47] It is worth noting that German critics are more used to listening to German dialogue delivered in received pronunciation (i.e. unaccented high German) and are accustomed to hearing German voices fairly neutrally dubbed in foreign-language films. In this cultural context, it is not surprising that Schygulla's vocal performance becomes part of her (anti-)star persona. As one commentator has suggested, 'it is the inimitable melody of her Bavarian idiom ... which singles her out from the bland chorus of high German'.[48]

Whity offers a particularly pertinent example of her vocal accomplishment in dialogue delivery.[49] This highly stylised, Western-derived melodrama ostensibly deals with slavery and the degenerate behaviour of a wealthy white rancher family. Several members of the family clan turn to Whity (Günther Kaufmann), the ill-treated illegitimate but devoted son and servant, to kill the others. In this scenario, Schygulla plays Hanna, a bar singer in love with Whity, and there is one scene in particular that showcases the actress's vocal dexterity as she ranges from gentle pleading, spitting sarcasm, vociferous hysteria to finally poignant resignation. Hanna is in her room getting ready for her performance in the saloon while trying to persuade Whity to leave his murderous and sadistic family and come away with her. She starts casually and cheerfully but then more warily delivers her invitation in a quiet voice, the lilt in her speech barely concealing her nervousness. This is offset by long pregnant pauses as she applies her lipstick. When Whity replies that he wants to stay with his family, she violently turns her head towards him in close-up and responds in a now strident, energetic voice, shaking her head and stabbing her chin forward with each word – 'You have no idea about your family' – only to follow this with an extended pause. Throughout her angry exchange with Whity, she breaks up the staccato of her over-modulated enunciation of each word, frequently pausing and making little noisy exhalations. Then, with a scornful chuckle and voice rising but still stressing each syllable, she snarls, 'You and your family!'

What is intriguing in this scene is Schygulla's use of gestures and movements, such as emphatic nodding, both to counterpoint and dramatise the semantic impact of her vocal delivery. Here she is able to use her lethargic style for dramatic effect by playing off the aural and visual registers, so that the slowness of one is balanced by greater animation in the other. She also modulates the variables of her voice (such as pitch, volume and rhythm) to dramatic effect despite maintaining the sluggish mode of vocal performance that by this time had come to characterise her somnambulistic persona.

Extending and consolidating the persona

It was while supporting Margit Carstensen (an outstanding theatrically trained actor) in the stylised high-camp drama *The Bitter Tears of Petra von Kant* that Schygulla began to find her Fassbinder roles both distasteful and limiting.[50] However, it was also in 1972 that she made her breakthrough in Germany in Fassbinder's five-part political 'Workers' Series' for television, *Eight Hours Are not a Day*. The series, set in a contemporary working-class milieu of factory floor and family, proved highly controversial with critics (both left and right-wing) but enormously successful with audiences due to its popular format and anti-capitalist ideology. Broadcast at primetime, it attracted audiences of 30 million, representing up to 65 per cent of overall viewing figures.[51] Working in television, Fassbinder shifted away from stylised genre allusions towards a more entertaining and accessible approach, including casting television stars. His new popular style not only adapted well to television but also virtually overnight transformed Schygulla, the erstwhile manneristic underground star, into a national star meriting media attention. As Marion, a middle-class office worker and fiancée to the working-class protagonist Jochen (played by Gottfried John), Schygulla won many more fans. The more naturalistic style adopted by the actors in *Eight Hours* was explicitly intended to attract a much wider viewing public than the educated and politicised minority audiences for Fassbinder's New German art-house films. In response to the unexpected popular success of the series, the influential weekly news journal *Der Spiegel* celebrated Schygulla's rise from 'super star of the subculture ... [to become] a beautiful concept for bourgeois art-lovers ... and ... a phenomenon in the current art scene'.[52] This first major article by Fritz Rumler on Schygulla, at the point of her transition from underground star towards mainstream stardom, described her career development with Fassbinder as culturally representative of the rebellious post-war generation. For Rumler, Schygulla was the one with 'whom a large section of the pop generation identifies', going on to state that

Critics pamper her like an idol, the aura of the born star seems to flicker around her curls. The subculture is a seismograph for moods and Schygulla demonstrates a few. She appears cool and artfully naïve, her moves are stylised and lethargic like a somnambulist, and the world which she traverses lies there loveless and very chaotic ... She is whore, diva, Sphinx, proletarian vamp, or an innocent backstreet Marilyn.[53]

Importantly, Rumler not only identified the hallmarks of her performance style but also coined the defining terms of Schygulla's star image. His comments further suggest that during this early period of her career she appealed more obviously to male spectators, functioning as an object of desire rather than as a figure for female identification. German critics (mostly male) insisted on claiming her as an indigenous Marilyn Monroe, partly because of her noted luminous screen image but also because of her naively innocent persona. Yet, at the same time, critics were also quick to note Schygulla's intelligence. For instance, Rumler, while drawing attention to the gap between Schygulla's image and her identity as a private person, quoted her as stating that 'The identity which one confers on me as a public person ... is not the identity which I give myself.'[54] Crucially, he pointed out that her comments were considered and intelligent. In later interviews, Schygulla would insist that as a highly educated person, she was the total opposite of a

Effi Briest (1974)

'backstreet Marilyn'.[55] Nevertheless, the tag had attached itself to her and it would be a long time before she was able to shake it off.

In the early 1970s, Schygulla consolidated her national stardom with a wider cinema audience through her role in *Effi Briest*, playing the eponymous nineteenth-century heroine who gets married when only seventeen to a much older aristocrat, Instetten (Wolfgang Schenck).[56] Here Schygulla's stylised performance of restraint (including her monotone whispered voice) is well suited, on a realist-historical level, to the polite ritualistic manners of the period. It is just as well suited to the formal requirements of the *mise en scène*. As a literary adaptation, it eschews realism in favour of baroque *mise en scène* and theatrical diction. The beautifully nuanced monochrome cinematography slowly fades to white and, with its iris effects, evokes daguerreotype photography of the period. The pace is extremely sedate, and often action and characters are circumscribed by lengthy intertitle quotations and verbatim passages from the novel, read in mellifluous voiceover by Fassbinder himself. The cinematography achieves a strong Sirkian sense of the entrapment and repression of its young heroine, tracking through an exquisite *mise en scène* of long, ornate tableaux and framing the characters in mirrors through lacy drapes, windows, doors and stairways.

Schygulla as Effi understates emotions, adapting the stylised lethargic acting (gestural and vocal) of her early roles as a 'backstreet Marilyn' to the equally stylised formal demands of playing the nineteenth-century heroine of a literary costume drama. Faced with presenting the all-pervasive auditory and visual confinement of Effi, Schygulla demonstrates her idiosyncratic actorly skill through the minutiae of small gestures (stirring a cup of tea to register displeasure) and facial expressivity (a slight tilt of her head, lowering her eyes, blinking or gazing focused or unfocused) that become a means of denoting her interiority. Here her 'less' is more. The authorial voiceover commentary informs us of Effi's feelings: 'Effi smiled to herself wistfully when remembering Crampas's description of Instetten.' Throughout this voiceover commentary she gazes obliquely out of the frame with her lips slightly apart, and as such her under-expressivity works to reveal none of the strong emotions one might expect to find simmering below the surface. Rather than illustrating the emotions evoked by the verbal commentary, Schygulla's visual performance of dreamy detachment means that any emotional impact is kept in abeyance, neither confirmed nor denied.

The film was released at the height of the women's liberation movement, and it is easy to understand why *Effi Briest*'s mode of narration, which keeps the heroine visually and aurally confined, rubbed against the early 1970s feminist zeitgeist of women's desire for self-determination. Fassbinder's rigorous formalism in *Effi Briest* provoked not only strong negative reactions from contemporary feminist reviewers and spectators but also from Schygulla, who could not identify with the role nor with his direction about how the character should be played (see below). Writing for the feminist *Frauen und Film*, ursula reuter-christiansen (*sic*) bluntly asserted that Effi is

twice abused ... once by her parents, husband and society; and second by a man who models her as obedient, perfect for testing out his own aesthetics. A woman who does not react ... [this is] real male-consumption ... what shall we do now with this effi briest of that time?[57]

Jill Forbes's review resonated with similar sentiments and, although a much more sophisticated and nuanced film critic, she too would have liked a film with more contemporary relevance – implicitly a more feminist update:

[I]t is a portrait of the artist much more than a portrayal of society. What Fassbinder has filmed is the author at work, rather than the work itself. And yet the film is beautiful to look at rather than psychologically compelling or politically significant.[58]

In general, male critics praised the film for its authorial faithfulness to Fontane rather than disliking it, and Peter Buchka praised it as a perfect authorial literary adaptation, because 'it makes you want to *read* again what you just have *seen*'.[59] He did, however, express some reservation about Schygulla's performance, 'as maybe a tad too enchanting and touching, a touch too elegiac and soft'.[60] Derek Elley admitted that it was a 'stunningly beautiful' film but he had also hoped for more than Effi's 'silent rage ... [and] meek acceptance of things capped by a final *cri du coeur*'.[61] While Mathes Rehder was generally ambivalent about the film, he unequivocally dismissed Schygulla's portrayal of Effi as 'sacrificial lamb ... Monotonously the novelist's words drip from her lips as if she already knew the ending from the beginning.'[62] More perceptively, the reviewer in *Le Monde* praised the film's delicate cinematography, its extremely refined diction and de-dramatisation while expressing dissatisfaction that it had not interrogated the Fontane novel.[63]

Although, a few years later, Schygulla and others would appreciate Fassbinder's rigorous formal control, at the time the overall feminist perspective of the female reviewers chimed with Schygulla's own view of the film. For her, *Effi Briest* should have depicted 'the dramatic battle of a young hot-blooded person who is driven out into the cold'. Instead, the film became 'a suffocating death in embroidered finery set in a gracious environment'.[64] The protracted shoot, and her disagreement with Fassbinder's directorial instructions to constrain and confine the character, culminated in an acrimonious separation. Fassbinder's approach emphasised formal innovation rather than telling a story and, thus, was 'fundamentally different' from Schygulla's. As Fassbinder later declared, 'I imposed what I wanted. ... She wanted the film to be ... about a woman towards the end of the nineteenth century and her problems ...'[65]

While still shooting *Effi Briest* in 1973, Schygulla made a public statement of her dissatisfaction with Fassbinder in one of the prestigious German colour supplements. In an article entitled 'I Didn't Want to Be His Doll Anymore', she stated that

At the centre of the 'anti-teater' is Fassbinder ... Around this kernel rest the others as independent parts. Where there is dependency there is submission and exploitation. Who exploits whom? This question is avoided. Altogether they produce *his* worldview. Each one adds their colour. In the beginning the colours were fresh.[66]

Of her cinematic and stage persona more generally, she noted:

The critics praised the amateurish quality. The amateurs became mannerists. The myth Fassbinder engendered the myth Schygulla: the angel from the backyard, the back-street Marilyn, the somnambulist of the no-man's land. She is the doll that moves – a useful invention for showing something, if we understand ourselves as an apparatus with a soul. Often I have been this doll. ... Now I want to lay her down ...[67]

I have left a room, but I have not yet closed the door behind me.[68]

Such statements clearly revealed the actress's frustrations with Fassbinder, providing clear evidence of an emerging rift between them.

Conclusion

Andrew Sarris wrote in his obituary of Fassbinder that 'It's hard to think of Fassbinder apart from the glowing image of Hanna Schygulla.'[69] Elsewhere, Sarris described Schygulla's early performance style as an 'extraordinary mixture of stylization, sensuality, passion, and disgust'.[70] This characterisation is richly suggestive as to why she was the perfect stylistic match for Fassbinder. There is certainly no doubt that between 1967 and 1974 Schygulla's inimitable manneristic and dilettantish performance style, including her vocal delivery, was symbiotic with Fassbinder's conception of cinema and, hence, was of structural significance in his developing oeuvre. Effectively, she was the essential 'play material' out of which he could develop his stylised vision.[71] However, in tension with Fassbinder's concept of ironic stylisation, Schygulla's gradual introduction of naturalism marked the beginnings of a departure between actor and director, muse and Svengali. After the actor's resistance to her director's stylised formalism became evident during the making of *The Bitter Tears of Petra von Kant*, Schygulla and Fassbinder diverged, culminating in a fundamental disagreement while making *Effi Briest*. Though the manneristic acting favoured by Fassbinder lay at the core of Schygulla's early star persona, she proved to be more versatile as an actor than the typical artificial figures she played in those

Fassbinder films that caught the imagination of the German critics. While it might be claimed that Schygulla probably would not have become a star without Fassbinder, her acting style was not *defined* by him, even though it developed with him during this formative period.

However, despite the emerging differences between Schygulla and Fassbinder during the early 1970s, and the professional rift that occurred after *Effi Briest*, 1974 did not mark the final break-up of their mutually beneficial professional relationship. It was, rather, a necessary break in a collaboration which, since *Petra von Kant*, had become fraught on a personal as much as on a professional front. Both were quite outspoken about this in later interviews. Fassbinder claimed, for instance, that he was getting tired of his star and muse, stating that 'Not to work with each other any more was a mutual decision. For Hanna it had a lot to do with the fact that at this point I found Margit Carstensen as fascinating as herself.'[72] Meanwhile, the erstwhile muse went on record as stating that she wanted to assert her independence and gain new experiences, insisting that 'What I initially had enjoyed, our idiosyncrasies, then became mannered. I [now] wanted something new. He could not invent something new for me, for this I needed to be myself, somebody different to ignite this in him.'[73] Although both explanations are retrospective, one can still accept them. What is certainly indisputable is that many Fassbinder collaborators found the director's demanding and irascible personality as repelling as compelling, forcing a break with him for either long or short periods. In this, Schygulla was typical of Fassbinder's coterie of actors. Yet in other ways she was different, approaching her work with analytical intelligence, as well as a desire to discover more about herself in the process. This made her an independent figure in Fassbinder's inner circle. It is for this reason that, while many critics have stressed Schygulla's dependence on Fassbinder as her Svengali, I have tried to show in this chapter how, by Fassbinder's own admission, 'the very

The glamorous anti-star in *Gods of the Plague* (1970)

existence of Hanna Schygulla was important for my work'.[74] In many ways, she was the life-blood vital to energise the heart of his work, and he certainly needed her particular anti-star aura to bring some low-life glamour to his early films.[75] But as well as taking her own career in new directions after 1974, Schygulla would also propel Fassbinder into new territory: namely, the mainstream and the international arena.

2 FROM 'BACKSTREET MARILYN' TO NEW MARLENE: THE RISE TO INTERNATIONAL FAME AS A STAR DIRECTED BY FASSBINDER, 1975–82

In the wake of domestic success and on the brink of international recognition, Schygulla, the muse, left Fassbinder, the director – a brave and unusual step for any star in the making. 'I drew a line under my career. That has saved it I think. To outsiders it looked as though I had reached my first career peak. *Effi Briest* became the first popular [cinema] success.'[1] She dropped out hippy-style, embarking on a quest of self-discovery and only intermittently accepted roles in theatre, television plays and a few films. Acting had now become predominantly a means of earning money for roaming through the USA and Mexico, the pursuit of yoga, teaching acting to kids, and painting.[2] In effect she became a 'jobbing' actor, with little concern about developing her star image or how the range of roles she accepted might affect her career. This chapter will briefly discuss the four-year break from Fassbinder, before considering in more detail Schygulla's subsequent meteoric rise to international stardom following a re-energised but also intensely problematic collaboration with him.

The 'jobbing' actor

Appropriately enough, Schygulla's first role after Fassbinder was as Therese, an actress in crisis, in Wim Wenders's *Wrong Move*.

The film, scripted by Peter Handke, was loosely based on Goethe's classic novel *Wilhelm Meister*, and forms the first part of Wenders's philosophical road-movie trilogy (the other two films being *Alice in den Städten/Alice in the Cities* [1973] and *Im Laufe der Zeit/Kings of the Road* [1976]), starring Rüdiger Vogler as a character in search of a German identity uncontaminated by fascism. Therese is Wilhelm's object of desire, one of a number of chance encounters along the way, who for a while become fellow travellers through Germany. Despite being an actress, Therese's image connotes 'naturalness', with her ash-blonde, slightly wavy shoulder-length hair and lack of any visible make-up. Consciously or otherwise, she is styled to erase the high artifice of Schygulla's established Fassbinder star image. Overall, Wenders's slow, contemplative pace is well suited to her performance style, but the difficult poetic and philosophical dialogue did make new demands on her declamatory skills, especially since *Wrong Move* was entirely filmed on location and recorded in direct sound with no possibility of subsequent studio retakes. In a four-minute naturalistically played scene, in which Therese is ironing and trying to learn her dialogue while Wilhelm types, she muses to herself about her acting fears, before directly addressing him. As her character speaks, her remarks parallel Schygulla's own attitudes to the extent that she appears to be self-conscious rather than merely self-reflexive. She explains that for her to perform 'without any feeling of suffocation' requires 'memory-work', so that she can claim the character's feelings as part of herself. Interestingly, in character as Therese, Schygulla articulates here the Method approach to acting. The sentiments expressed by the fictional character are, implicitly at least, also comments about Schygulla's changing attitude and register an increasing distancing from her earlier Brechtian anti-acting style.

Several critics noted how the film's mode of narration enabled 'a corporeal and emotional freedom for all its actors', and praised the film for its understated ensemble acting. Hans-C. Blumenberg, for instance, commented on the ensemble of actors, regarding them as being 'freed from all routine'.[3] However, Wenders, in his DVD director's commentary of 2002 (i.e. seventeen years later), confessed that, although he 'adored' Schygulla, he 'didn't have Fassbinder's outstanding skill in directing actors', which he felt made her appear 'wooden'. This opinion, however, was not expressed in the contemporary reviews of the film. Indeed, Schygulla was judged as perfectly suited to playing Therese as an actor in crisis, even though (for other reasons) she was not wholly able to make that role her own. For instance, the direct-sound recording of poetic-philosophical dialogue exchanges apparently strained against her otherwise naturalistic performance style, itself a marker of how far Fassbinder's influence still lingered over her screen image.

Schygulla's next film broke more decidedly with her 'backstreet Marilyn' image. Directed by Vojtěch Jasný, *Ansichten eines Clowns/The Clown* (1976) is a literary adaptation of Heinrich Böll's famous 1960s novel about a wealthy Protestant dropout, Hans (Helmut Griem), who loves a working-class Catholic woman, Marie

The development of a more naturalistic
screen persona

(Schygulla). The story of their problematic relationship, break-up
and Hans's self-pitying descent into alcoholic poverty is told through
subjective flashbacks from his point of view. *The Clown* was released
in the wake of Volker Schlöndorff's topical and internationally
acclaimed *The Lost Honor of Katharina Blum* (1975), also based on a
Böll novel, and suffered critically by comparison. The story was
considered both verbose and literary, even outdated with its religious
theme and political focus on generational conflict: namely, the son
confronting his parents with their fascist past.

Schygulla's performance received mixed reviews, although many
critics were full of praise for the lovers' tender first night together.
In this touching scene, she erased the screen persona of the
knowingly sexy 'backstreet Marilyn' altogether. Drawing on a
repertoire of naturalistic gestures and looks, she convincingly

portrays a chaste and deeply religious young woman who is caught up in a play of hesitations and yearnings for the man she loves. For example, in response to his desiring look, she modestly tightens her dressing gown across her chest and, while sharing a cigarette, nervously puffs on it like a non-smoker. In the main, however, the reviews would have done little to reassure her that she could be an acclaimed actor without Fassbinder.

The return to Fassbinder and international breakthrough: *The Marriage of Maria Braun*

It is unlikely that Schygulla would have become an international star if Fassbinder had not re-established contact in 1978, offering her (quite out of the blue) the starring role in *The Marriage of Maria Braun*. Originally, this film was intended as a 'cheap quickie' to fill a production gap before embarking on the mega production of *Berlin Alexanderplatz*, although it eventually assumed far more importance.[4] Initially, the much more famous Romy Schneider had been the producers' first choice but, by all accounts, star and director did not hit it off. Schygulla has frequently commented that serendipity was a governing principle of her career, and it certainly played a part in her being offered the eponymous role in *The Marriage of Maria Braun*. However, it was her scintillating performance that would make this role her most iconic, locating it at the undisputed core of her star persona, and it seems pointless to speculate whether or not it would have been as successful with Romy Schneider. Indeed, it is hard to imagine anyone else as Maria Braun, for, as one reviewer proclaimed, 'Maria Braun is Hanna Schygulla!'[5]

Since Schygulla had last worked with him, Fassbinder had become internationally renowned as an outstanding auteur. During the same period, her experience as a 'jobbing' actor had been underwhelming, effectively dissipating some of the star power she had accumulated under Fassbinder's direction. Thus, when shooting on *Maria Braun* started in early 1978, their professional relationship had changed and was far from equal. The shoot was extremely tense, largely because Fassbinder's heavy drug habit made him increasingly volatile, a situation exacerbated later the same year by the suicide of his former lover Armin Meier.

The film starts in 1943 with the heroine's marriage (literally amidst exploding bombs) to Hermann (Klaus Löwitsch), after which they spend just one whole night and half a day together before he returns to the front. Waiting for him, she survives the war, but when Hermann is reported dead, she has an affair with Bill (George Byrd), a gentle black GI, whom she kills when her husband suddenly returns. Hermann subsequently takes the blame for the murder and is imprisoned, while Maria promises to wait for him and sets out to make a fortune for them both. Thanks to her outstanding business acumen, she makes herself indispensable to her boss, the industrialist Oswald (Ivan Desny), and they become lovers, although each month she visits her husband in prison, telling all. When Hermann is released, he goes abroad to make his own fortune and returns only after Oswald's sudden death. To her great surprise and shock, she discovers that Oswald had made a deal with Hermann for him to disappear until after his own imminently anticipated death. It dawns on Maria that she has not been in control of the life whose happy outcome she had 'postponed' until the long-awaited reunion with Hermann. In the kitchen of the new house she has had built for them both, she lights her cigarette on the gas cooker and blows out the open flame, while Hermann listens to the 1954 world cup final commentary on the radio. As the delirious radio voice screams that Germany has beaten Hungary, Maria lights a match and the house blows up. The film has come full circle, from the opening explosions to the final one, but it remains unclear whether this last explosion was intentional or not. Interestingly, the ambiguous art-house ending was devised at Schygulla's insistence, because she was not convinced that the go-getting Maria Braun would intentionally kill herself and Hermann in a car accident (as specified in the screenplay); for once, Fassbinder let himself be persuaded. Elsewhere, the script worked to the actor's advantage, with some mordantly witty dialogue by Peter Märthesheimer[6] and Pea Fröhlich, enabling Schygulla to create both a feisty and charming character. Michael Ballhaus's superb lighting and camerawork revealed the actor at her best in a succession of sexy and glamorous costumes (including lacy black underwear), all of which resulted in an award-winning performance.

Often moving beyond psychological realism, Schygulla plays her multifaceted role in ways that invoke a protagonist shaped by cinematic and historical references, one that acquires an allegorical status. Maria's unfolding career and ensuing emotional numbness, for instance, can be read as loosely paralleling stages of the West 'German economic miracle', which in turn was based on disavowal of guilt. Her allegorical function is foregrounded explicitly in one particular scene when she refers to herself as the 'Mata Hari of the economic miracle'. These various allegorical and cinematic tropes feed into and coexist in a nuanced psychological portrayal of a rounded character living through the post-war period. Film scholar Johannes von Moltke regarded her, like many other critics, as representing 'German history itself', stating that 'Not only ... is she the quintessential woman of the 1940's or 1950's [sic] ... but she is seen to literally *embody* Germany, becoming a "Germania" of the New German Cinema.'[7]

In von Moltke's case study of Schygulla, however, he also links her performance to that of the drag impersonator, foregrounding 'construction, theatricality, and artifice' as key elements. Drawing on the perception of Schygulla as a gay icon, he problematises the allegorical critical consensus by claiming that unlike other portrayals of female protagonists with allegorical potential in New German Cinema,[8] 'the more intractable histrionics of [Schygulla's] performance' extend *beyond* allegory, arguing that '[Schygulla's] embodiment is marked, like the parodies of the drag performer, by excess: she is not simply a woman of the fifties, but one who is constantly playing a woman of the fifties'.[9]

It is a persuasive proposition, one which explains her iconic gay status, but it does not acknowledge her undoubted attraction also to other types of spectator. For example, in one scene Maria/Schygulla adopts a familiar pose, pouting in front of a mirror, applying the heavy theatrical make-up and piling up the poodle-like curls. Together with Betti Klenze (Elisabeth Trissenaar), she sings Zarah Leander's famous 1940s hit 'Not to Cry Because of Love'. This imitation of the glamorous Ufa star functions, I would argue, polysemically.[10] It works, on the one hand, as a camp reference for some gay people (in other words, as 1970s actors playing 1950s protagonists posing as 1940s divas), while simultaneously putting an image of two attractive women (Schygulla and Trissenaar) on display for the heterosexual gaze. At the same time, it also operates in terms of nostalgic memory for some of the older people in the audience. Such multiple spectator attractions are often evident in *Maria Braun*, allowing Schygulla to differentially impress the audience with her incandescent screen presence.

Due to their revitalised collaboration, Fassbinder staged his star more glamorously than ever before, Schygulla seizing every chance to show her distinct acting ability and performance range. Her characteristic performance style effortlessly combined being in character as the psychologically rounded Maria Braun *and* being herself, while also referencing other films of the period. In doing so, she evoked the resonating German stereotype of the *Trümmerfrau*, the women whose indestructible spirit literally rebuilt the future out of the rubble of war-ravaged buildings.[11] She further combined this symbol of female survival and strength with that of a multifaceted heroine who is not only quick-witted and resourceful but also ruthlessly efficient in the pursuit of her goal to accumulate as much wealth as possible for her husband's return once she knows he is

Multiple spectator attractions: with Elisabeth
Trissenaar in *The Marriage of Maria Braun* (1979)

alive. This added up to a powerful and unique female identity that
henceforth became her most iconic persona.

The various complexities of the Schygulla persona manifest
themselves in a number of scenes in *Maria Braun*. For instance, after
the war, while Maria's husband remains missing, she has to survive
by taking a bar job with the American occupying forces. In a
sequence consisting of two scenes, her mother and Betti have already
learned from Willi (Betti's husband, who has just returned from the
front) that Hermann has been reported dead. Weeping, they agonise
over how to break the news to Maria. She arrives at the darkly lit
family kitchen loaded with goods only to discover that her friend
Willi has come home. Overcome with joy, she embraces him and the
others, unaware of the impending news. As she stands with her back
to the camera, cooling her wrist under the running water tap, Willi
suddenly and directly, even brutally, tells Maria of her husband's

death. With her back still to the camera, she holds her gestures in abeyance before violently spinning round and then ducking down to propel herself out of the house. Followed by her mother, Maria declares that she is going to the bar because she needs to be alone. In the next shot, she approaches her admirer Bill on the dimly lit dance floor, and, with a courteous bow and a grave voice, asks him in English, 'Will you dance with me, Mr Bill?' He grasps her in a tight but comforting embrace and they remain so, barely moving to Glenn Miller's 'Moonlight Serenade'. In a constrained, low voice, she explains, 'My man is dead', before the camera pulls back so that they are subsumed among the dancing crowd.

Schygulla's pervasive lethargy is put to great emotional effect in this sequence. In typical Schygulla fashion, Maria's reaction to the news of her husband's death is principally conveyed through emotional understatement and lethargic corporeality (through a heavy-bodied movement), broken only and startlingly as she violently spins round before rushing out of the house. In a perverse reversal, the typical signs of grief are expressed here by the other actors, so that Maria/Schygulla starts the scene with tears of joy at Willi's homecoming, followed by emotional numbness at the devastating news, and finishes with the consoling, enveloping embrace of another man. Schygulla's performance style does not necessarily require the external signs of emotion, as her grief is a narrative given. To put it differently, her limited facial and gestural expressivity are both embedded and anticipated in the process of narration and, thus, her understatement can suggest (as the neutral figures in the Kuleshov experiments) greater emotional complexity than a more ostentatious style of acting. What is different from her earlier and often deliberately dilettantish performance in Fassbinder's films is the unforced manner in which shifts in emotional expressions are calibrated to the scale of her signature acting style. However, this time they convey psychological depth rather than merely appearing formally stylised. Schygulla's maturing style demonstrates above all her outstanding intelligence as a performer. Due to this distinctly idiosyncratic style, her limited expressive gestural range is not apparent, nor is it at the expense of its affective potential.

Elsewhere, however, Schygulla's acting shifts through a range of registers to simultaneously conform to a more conventional Hollywood-style screen persona *and* remain that of a German type, having both contemporary appeal *and* historical resonance while, finally, also combining psychological depth with allegorical abstraction. After the disclosure of Hermann's death, Maria has started a relationship with Bill and is now pregnant. Bantering in English and German as they look forward to bringing up their child bilingually, they enter Maria's family home and, finding that the rest of the family is away, undress each other playfully, evidently quite at ease in their sexual directness. Schygulla's performance here has a purposefulness and lightness of movement rather than the lethargic sexual responsiveness she displays in earlier Fassbinder films. Entering the bedroom, Bill's face is marked by a foreboding shadow. While the door remains ajar, Maria (wearing a lacy black slip and silk stockings) playfully pushes the big naked Bill onto the bed. At this point, we see a gaunt and unkempt Hermann in uniform lurking in the open door frame observing their love play. Finally, as Bill kisses Maria on the shoulder, he also notices the figure, and then, in close-up with her lover to the right, Maria gazes out of the frame towards the door, saying in a quiet and incredulous voice, 'Hermann?' Turning to Bill, she continues quietly, now in a matter-of-fact voice: 'Look Bill! That is Hermann, my husband.' A smile appears on her lips as, with relief, she exhales a softly drawn-out 'Ahhh', and laughs. She then moves towards the hovering figure, only to receive a violent slap across the face that knocks her to the floor. A horrified Bill shouts 'Maria' and steps forward. He looks at Hermann, who gazes past both of them to focus on a packet of cigarettes on the bedroom table. Lighting one, he inhales it greedily. In the meantime, with the room suffused in slanted chiaroscuro lighting, Bill picks Maria up as she rests against his chest. This medium shot is followed immediately by a medium-long profile shot of Hermann, who is still avoiding their gaze while smoking intently. He then turns round, inspecting the rumpled sheets and, with a sudden explosive surge of rage, rips them apart. Bill wrestles with Hermann in an attempt to restrain him, while the husband seems to suppress a sob. Meanwhile, Maria watches them both with an inscrutable expression, her body half raised from the floor. Then, trance-like, she stands up, slowly reaching behind her to pick up a bottle, and hits Bill over the head, watching him collapse. In close-up, we see Maria's face, its features obscured in shadow except for her parted lips and bright blue eyes. Finally, Hermann turns round to lock eyes with his wife, as Maria exhales with pleasure before her lips slightly tighten, seemingly expressing satisfaction with the resolution. The scene ends with a cut to the US military trial for Bill's murder.

The unexpected return of Hermann, who witnesses his wife in a new sexual and loving relationship, evokes the generic German *Trümmerfilm*. Here, the unforeseen late return of a POW often leads to the realisation that another man has taken his place, a familiar dramatic trope that is born out of actual historical events. Additionally, beyond the powerful historical and cinematic resonances that this sudden twist of fate would have had for many older Germans, visually and thematically the scene alludes to Sirkian melodrama[12] and to Hollywood's use of film noir chiaroscuro lighting conventions to express the amoral sexual figure of the femme fatale.

It is striking how this scene evokes Schygulla's persona from previous Fassbinder films. Her state of semi-undress and the sudden, brutal slap across her face are two very familiar tropes. However, in this instance, the slap is more than a gestural citation from B-movies (as, for instance, in *Love Is Colder than Death*), because it is also specifically character-motivated. In her transition from joyous recognition of Hermann to somnambulistic assault on Bill, and culminating in her pleasurable sigh when the estranged husband and

Expressionistic and Hollywood film noir
lighting compose the femme fatale

wife finally exchange looks, Schygulla plays off naturalistic acting
(Maria's and Bill's sexual bantering) against her stylised lethargy and
under-expressivity, punctuating both with recognisable Schygulla
mannerisms, such as her inimitable laugh. It is not only the
cinematography but also Schygulla's acting here that holds in balance
generic references to 1950s Hollywood melodrama and film noir, on
the one hand, and the 1940s German *Trümmerfilm*, on the other.
The scene reveals how her performance style is still sufficiently
stylised to reference her earlier star image, even though this is now
enhanced with a new, more vivacious and modulated mode of acting.
As such, she both conforms to the psychological realism of
Hollywood/mainstream cinema acting, while simultaneously
appealing to those familiar with her image.

Another, very different, scene illustrates what makes her so
appealing to an international audience. This is Maria's opportunistic
encounter with Oswald on the train. Having just aborted Bill's child,
Maria is returning home. Boarding an overcrowded train, she notices
a first-class sign and a flicker of a smile plays around her mouth as

she starts shouting 'Leni', pushing through the crowd as she pretends to search for her daughter. Arriving in the empty first-class carriage, she asks the conductor how far she can travel with the money she has. During this brief exchange, Maria discovers that a wealthy French-German émigré businessman is the only first-class occupant. Quick-wittedly, she passes her suitcase to the conductor, making him her accomplice. He passes her clothes and make-up as she disappears into the toilet, changing into a seductive black dress and fishnet stockings, while applying glamorous make-up and attending to her hair. She thanks him with a kiss and a wink before approaching the passenger, who is reading a book, asking him in English, with a radiant smile, whether the seat opposite is available. As he doesn't understand English, Maria repeats her question in German. He confirms that it is free and introduces himself as Dr Karl Oswald. As she sits down and closes her eyes, she looks very alluring. Oswald is distracted from his book and tries to engage her in conversation, but she responds only monosyllabically before telling him bluntly that she wants some peace and quiet to think. While he continues to scrutinise her, a drunk black GI (Günther Kaufmann) enters the compartment swearing loudly, 'Fucking old train, fucking old Germany …'. When Oswald remonstrates with him that the lady wants to sleep, the GI notices Maria and, commenting on her beauty, asks her, 'What about fucking?' She responds in German-accented English, with her eyes still closed, 'To answer your question, I'm really the best one you could ever be fucked by, but you'll never get the chance after I've kicked your bloody old prick and your bloody old balls drop off!' On the last word, she opens her eyes to glare at him before standing up and announcing, 'And now, sir, you'd better fuck off immediately or I'll be forced to report you to the military police to get you bloody old son of a bitch into jail.' An impressed non-English-speaking Oswald asks her, 'Where did you learn such good English?' 'In bed,' she replies.

In comparison to the earlier Fassbinder films with their often more stilted dialogue, it is easy to see why such feisty language, along with traditional comic reversal structures, would appeal to a broader and more international audience. Maria's plucky opportunistic attempt to get herself a new job with Oswald here seems admirable. Similarly, there is plenty to amuse and admire in her play with the drunk GI, abruptly shifting from seeming lasciviousness to confident control. On its own, however, Schygulla's sexy screen image might not have been enough to bring about international fame even with such splendidly nuanced acting. Instead, this came about due to an extraordinary set of circumstances that made *Maria Braun* a much more important film than anyone had originally anticipated.

At the time, Fassbinder believed that the high-budget *Eine Reise ins Licht/Despair* (1978) would provide him with an international commercial breakthrough to match his artistic ones, largely due to the film's international cast that included Dirk Bogarde and Andréa Ferréol, as well as the original English script by Tom Stoppard (based on Vladimir Nabokov's well-known novel).[13] However, to his amazement, when *Despair* was entered in the official Cannes Film Festival competition in May 1978, it flopped. Shrewd, as always, Fassbinder had an answer print of *Maria Braun* flown in and quickly organised a private screening for the potential distributors, even though the film was still in post-production.[14] By all accounts, this impromptu screening received a standing ovation and resulted in an almost immediate worldwide interest for distribution rights (including, eventually, twenty-five countries).

In February 1979, *Maria Braun* was officially premiered as the opening film at the Berlin Film Festival, where it was unanimously praised as a masterpiece, earning Schygulla a Silver Berlin Bear but no award for Fassbinder. Schygulla subsequently went on to win Germany's most prestigious Filmband in Gold, along with many other international awards.[15] Concurrent with the festival, the German weekly *Der Stern* featured many glamour shots of Schygulla

This image of the family gathering featured as a
still in many West German reviews

wearing her 1950s-style costumes as illustrations to Gerhard
Zwerenz's post-novelisation and serialisation of *Maria Braun*.
The general media hype promised a more commercially orientated
film and, indeed, when it was theatrically released a month later it
had excellent attendances, still showing after thirty-one weeks in
Frankfurt and twenty-eight weeks in Berlin.[16]

In the context of German critical reception, the most widely
discussed aspect of *Maria Braun* was the historical dimension,
particularly its attention to period detail and its depiction of
recognisable family situations, such as post-war deprivations and
estranged men returning home. Additionally, as part of their
reviews, critics acclaimed it as Fassbinder's German Hollywood
film, praising the ensemble acting and waxing lyrical over
Schygulla's performance, which was lauded as being 'foremost
amongst all the actors ... never clichéd';[17] 'sparklingly erotic',[18]

'an exceptional achievement'.[19] Wolfram Schütte, a leading critic, considered Schygulla 'an incarnation of a whole generation of women ... who manages to convey this through her gestures and disposition'.[20] Among the many rave reviews, the following capture the tone and range of the praise: 'The outstanding actress ... shows the tragedy [of a life deferred]'[21] and 'plays the eponymous heroine with fascinating coldness'.[22] 'Inimitable ... to reverse the famous advertising slogan – Maria Braun is Hanna Schygulla!'[23] A year later, Fassbinder's only film ever to go on general release in the GDR was praised by East German reviewers for Schygulla's realistic acting, one critic insisting that 'How she manages to depict the withering of emotions, how she conveys weakness and self-assurance, and how she renders visible vulgarity and sensuality – that is style.'[24]

Due to the enthusiastic reception at Cannes and in West Germany, the film attracted Hollywood majors and in 1980 led to an expensive publicity and promotion campaign in the United States, including preview screenings.[25] Unlike the more sober German poster, which merely featured Maria's head in semi-profile towering over the heads of Hermann and Oswald, in the United States the film was promoted with a provocatively alluring poster depicting Schygulla with legs parted, fastening her stocking straps and gazing obliquely over her shoulder. Here she is all in black, with high heels, stockings, sexy corset and a cute little feathered hat on top of her tumbling curls. According to J. Hoberman, the poster sold more tickets than the rave reviews by 'smitten' New York critics.[26] Schygulla made personal appearances during the promotional tour and was invited to the film's opening premiere at the New York Film Festival in October 1979, where she gave many interviews. This intensity of promotion, which centred largely around its star rather than its director, was a first for a Fassbinder film,[27] not only underpinning the ensuing art-house commercial success but also helping to produce a more favourable critical reception.

The black and white GDR poster is remarkable in its
starkness; the West German poster connotes historical
drama; the famous sexy poster seduced and beckoned
international audiences

Eventually, however, Schygulla would pay a high price for this shift in media attention from director to star (as discussed below).

After Schygulla's massive exposure at the New York Film Festival, American critics outdid each other in praising her riveting performance and sex appeal. Foremost among them was David Denby's eulogy:

The tantalizing and insolent beauty Hanna Schygulla has appeared in many [Fassbinder] films ... but she never had a role as plummy as [this one] ... With her bee-stung lips, poodle-cut blond hair, and blood-raising sensual fullness, Schygulla is one of the ripest and funniest screen images in years – an improbable cross between Dietrich and Harlow ... As Schygulla plays it, the role is a series of risks and provocations. She raises screen acting to a new level of sexual knowingness.[28]

Vincent Canby similarly commented on how her 'brilliantly complex performance' holds the film together:

[She] is the kind of enchanted actress who, at any one moment in a Fassbinder movie, is the sum of all its parts, plus a little more ... she effectively represents everything it's about. This ... has as much to do with her looks and gestures as it does with the mechanics of a particular performance. Whatever it is, it's splendid and mysterious.[29]

Due to her 'enigmatic sensuality', Schygulla was compared by one critic to Greta Garbo,[30] while other reviewers discussed her in less discreet art-house terms, one stating that 'I can't say whether Schygulla is a great actress but she is definitely 1979's steamiest on-screen-turn-on.'[31]

Success is only ever relative, however, and New York (where the film ran for fifty-four weeks[32]) is not the United States, as Dan Talbot (foreign film importer and film critic) pointed out: 'A hit foreign film, like *Maria Braun*, will still only have 200 dates across

Schygulla's enigmatic smile – 'inviting and forbidding' (L. Kardish)

the country. It's not even in the same league with a mild Hollywood hit.'[33] Some critics (especially New York-based Canby) expected Schygulla to be nominated, if not to win, the Oscar but, despite all the hype, this came to nothing. The film wasn't even nominated. Instead, Volker Schlöndorff's *Die Blechtrommel/The Tin Drum* won the Oscar for foreign-language film in 1979. The film was, however, nominated for the Hollywood Foreign Press Association's 1979 Golden Globe Award for foreign-language films, although again it failed to win.

In other 'territories', *Maria Braun* had broadly positive reviews. On its release in France, in January 1980, the film was acclaimed by critics and widely reviewed as the 'biggest commercial German film success since the war'.[34] As for Schygulla, 'everyone adores her', claimed Gérard Courant.[35] Jean-Philippe Domecq applauded her ability to incarnate the role 'with captivating charm ... and tactile sensuality',[36] while Jean de Baroncelli praised her 'superb interpretation'.[37] Meanwhile, on its British release in September 1980, the film went on to become the autumn's top-running non-English-

The 'sensual and sensational' emerging
international star

language film.[38] Critical praise for the film was more qualified, with
many reviewers finding the political and allegorical parallels too
obscure and forced. Schygulla's performance, however, was hailed as
magnificent, sensual and sensational. As in the United States, her
luminous beauty was often commented on, with Alan Brien's review
incorporating the most in terms of enthusiastic purple prose:

With the faintly fleshy, naively corrupt face of a Renaissance cupid, and the
Blue-Angel body of a Dietrich ... here she emerges from the chrysalis of
[Fassbinder's] screen repertory company and takes off as an international star
... [She] never puts a black-stockinged foot wrong as, perkily sexy and
chummily ruthless, she treads the minefield of the first post-war decade, and
all the parallel trails are trodden with perfectly observed precision.[39]

International reception revealed a consensus that Schygulla had
become a world star, as *Variety* reported: '[She] has become the most

sought after German actress.'[40] Interestingly, rather than the typical scenario whereby a successful art film turned an actor into a star, in this case it would be more accurate to claim that the film became a worldwide art-house success largely due to Schygulla's compelling screen persona. At this time, the loss of star power that she had suffered during the 'interregnum' years away from Fassbinder was more than compensated for by the reviews she received for *Maria Braun*. Indeed, for a while it seemed as though the star had even eclipsed her director in terms of broad media acclaim.

The 'offering' of a young rival: *Berlin Alexanderplatz*

Before *Maria Braun* was released in spring 1979, Schygulla continued working with other directors, appearing in two television films. Afterwards, she returned to Fassbinder to make *Die dritte Generation/The Third Generation* (1979), a biting and bitter satire about German terrorists in which she played an important ensemble role. However, this did not significantly enhance her screen persona. More noteworthy was her role in Fassbinder's literary adaptation of Alfred Döblin's modernist classic *Berlin Alexanderplatz* (1980). This fifteen-and-a-half-hour television series, which was subsequently released in cinemas, was set against the grinding poverty that characterised the underbelly of the hedonistic 'Weimar' years of the late 1920s. The film narrates the epic struggles of ex-convict Franz Biberkopf (Günter Lamprecht), pimp and petty criminal, who vows to become henceforth an honest man after being released from a penitentiary for the manslaughter of a lover. Schygulla plays the part of Eva, a high-class prostitute and Franz's loyal ex-lover and guardian angel. However, it was the younger Barbara Sukowa who took the leading female role of Mieze, the great love of the naively lumpen Biberkopf.[41] Despite appearances in twelve out of the fourteen episodes, Schygulla's name only appeared at the end of the credits, as though she was simply making a guest appearance.

In the context of Schygulla's star construction, there is a scene of particular symbolic interest that merits further discussion.[42] In this episode, Eva and her flash pimp visit a lonely Biberkopf, who has survived betrayal and attempted murder, leaving him maimed with only one arm. To cheer him up, Eva has 'maternally' befriended Mieze, a young prostitute, and asked her to take care of her beloved Biberkopf. Somewhat reluctantly, he agrees to her 'gift' of a companion. However, when he meets the sweetly naive Mieze, he is immediately captivated by her irresistible innocent charm. With hindsight, it is the oedipal power configurations of this romantic triangular relationship that is so striking, this complicated scenario being further compounded later on when Mieze offers Biberkopf's sexual services so that Eva can have a child. Added to this already complex situation is the well-known fact that Biberkopf was an identity often claimed by Fassbinder as his alter-ego. Hence, the diegetic event whereby Biberkopf receives the young lover and rival from the older maternal woman acquires added significance due to the extra-diegetic fact that it was Sukowa rather than Schygulla who was critically feted on the film's release, with Sukowa winning the German Best Young Actress award. The oedipal exchange of Mieze as Eva's offering to her ex-lover foreshadowed not only the decline of German critical acclaim for Schygulla but also the fact that Sukowa would soon upstage her as the new star in Fassbinder's universe. Despite all expectations, it was the vigorous Sukowa rather than the languid Schygulla who went on to play the eponymous central character in *Lola* (1981) in the second part of Fassbinder's historical FRG (Federal Republic of Germany) trilogy. In 2004, Günter Rohrbach, the producer of many Fassbinder's films, noted that

[This] actress could have become dangerous for Schygulla in the world of [Fassbinder] ... It looked at the time as if Fassbinder and Schygulla had finally had enough of each other ... What had once appeared as his symbiotic attachment to Schygulla his star had now become destructive.[43]

Indeed, in 1980, during the long shoot of *Berlin Alexanderplatz* that lasted from June 1979 to April 1980, Fassbinder became tired of Schygulla. Furthermore, this was at the very point when it became patently obvious that she was getting most of the American media attention for *Maria Braun*.

A reversal of power at a high price: *Lili Marleen*

Berlin Alexanderplatz would have been their last film together had it not been for Schygulla's new-found international star status, which resulted in her being offered the leading role in the most expensive German production of the post-war era (DM 10.5 million) by the commercial producer Luggi Waldleitner.[44] Schygulla accepted the title role in *Lili Marleen* on condition that Fassbinder would direct her rather than one of the old guard. Previously, when Schygulla and Fassbinder resumed their collaboration, her star power had been on the wane. Now, however, she was in a position to appoint Fassbinder as her director of choice. Surprisingly, despite their fraught relationship, he accepted. This was even more surprising, since not only had the film's scriptwriter previously blocked funding for a cherished project[45] but also its producer was better known for making reactionary porn rather than art films.[46]

It is ironic that Fassbinder's former anti-star would achieve her most popular international success starring in a film about a politically compromised singer who made her dazzling career in the shadow of the swastika. Based on Lale Andersen's fictionalised autobiography, *Lili Marleen* traces the singer's meteoric rise to fame following the popularity of the song 'Lili Marleen' with both British and German soldiers. While the film charts the increasing success of the song in its world war setting, it also centres on the doomed love story of a mediocre German cabaret singer, Willie (Schygulla), and classical musician Robert Mendelssohn (Giancarlo Giannini). Mendelssohn is not only Swiss Jewish but he is also responsible for smuggling Jews out of Germany for the Resistance, which is headed by his wealthy father (Mel Ferrer). To further her career, Willie ignores political realities, announcing that her hugely successful song 'is only a song', and it is only towards the end of the film that she puts herself in danger by helping the Jewish Resistance.

Along with its mixed international cast, the film itself is a dynamic hybrid. It combines (both thematically and aesthetically) Hollywood with Nazi films, with Sirkian melodrama and 1940s-style musical sequences sitting alongside the extravagant sentimental and nationalistic Ufa melodramas and musical *Revuefilms*. For many critics, the film was compromised by this aesthetic range. Nevertheless, as a spectacular musical based on a popular song, as well as being a historical biopic, *Lili Marleen* was aimed squarely at the international market (the USA, in particular), and for this reason was shot in English and later dubbed and subtitled into German.[47] Playing the role of a Third Reich star, Schygulla received the full Ufa glamour treatment. As a result, she was shown more often in close-up than ever before. Analogous to her role as Maria Braun, where her career had paralleled German economic historical development, here Willie's showbiz vocation was presented as an exemplary Third Reich career. Yet, unlike his commercial producer, Fassbinder was interested in both depicting *and* undermining the myth of the song, highlighting the perverse but banal glamour of the Ufa films that had been such a major part of the popular appeal of fascism in the 1930s and 1940s. For him, the key issue was Willie's determination to succeed in her career in show business irrespective of the socio-historical context, whereas for Schygulla that aspect of the scenario needed to be balanced with the emotional pull of the love story.[48]

The facile *Ersatz* glamour of the Nazi diva

For the first time, singing was crucial to Schygulla's performance, particularly as she had to reprise the same song over and over again in varied styles, performing different kinds of pastiche. Her first scene as a cabaret singer is in English and it quite clearly pays homage to the Hollywood musical. It is a light-hearted song and tap-dance number performed with great gusto by Schygulla in a jolly pink polka-dotted dress and a big bow in her hair. She sings in a light soprano and nearly accent-free English, waving her arms in the air, clicking her fingers, wiggling her hips and tapping her feet – resembling, in other words, an emblematic hoofer. This lively number, which attracts the admiration of a Nazi official, is pleasingly performed by Willie/Schygulla. Crucially, however, it functions in this carefree manner precisely in order to contrast with a series of subsequent 'Lili Marleen' performances, as does another brief intimate singing and tap-dance routine a few minutes later.

In her first rendition of the theme song, Willie is no longer animated but rigid with nerves as she sings to an audience in a pub. Wearing a satin pink dress and assuming a familiar Schygulla pose (legs parted but not provocatively), she barely moves her outstretched arms, placing her hands either firmly on her hips or clasping them behind her back, all the time gently swaying rather than swinging her hips. When she starts to sing, her vocal performance is in stark contrast to the earlier light-hearted English-language song, the delivery taking on the characteristic style of *Sprechgesang*, an expressive form of vocal articulation that shifts between speech and singing. While her pitch alternates between mezzo and soprano, she drawls out certain last syllables in a dramatic staccato manner, embellishing others with an arabesque trill. The effect of this intonation is that Schygulla self-consciously performs a bad Marlene Dietrich imitation in a voice that is noticeably higher and more bland than the original, lacking Dietrich's famous smoky-gravelly timbre. Willie doesn't get very far through her song before the local Bavarian punters disrupt her with rude comments about her legs being better than her voice; as a result, she has to finish the song against the noise of an ensuing pub brawl, which eventually drowns her out.

In a subsequent gala performance of the song, Schygulla sings in a mezzo-soprano voice, in a manner that, although melodious, is rather anodyne. This refers directly to the style of the original singer, Lale Andersen. Singing in the vast auditorium of the Olympic stadium, Willie has now reached her zenith as an entertainer, due to the fact that her recording of the song is broadcast daily by Radio Belgrade to German and Allied soldiers on the battle fronts. Framed by swastika banners and dressed in a glitzy blue evening gown, she emerges into the spotlight from the dial of a gigantic wireless. She then descends the broad stairway slowly and rather gingerly, holding the long train of her dress in one hand. During this performance, Willie is quite animated, smiling and bowing, extending her arms towards her adoring public. This scene unfolds with an ironic montage that juxtaposes close-ups of Willie on stage with the live broadcasting of her performance to the soldiers at the battle front, the tossing of flowers onto the stage cross-cut with images of bodies thrown into the air.

Willie's next stage appearance reinvokes the Marlene performance style with a visual pastiche of the famous Lola in Sternberg's *Blue Angel*, featuring Dietrich's signature top hat and slashed long black dress that reveals her shapely legs, with the addition of a big, campy golden bow around her neck and another one positioned strategically to accentuate her crotch (see image on p. ii).[49] This brief scene is composed of rapid close-ups and medium-long shots intercut with the Gestapo discovering Robert's identity. On this occasion, Willie sings 'Lili Marleen' in an upbeat, brassy military marching style that finishes with a high 'Laaa, laaa, laaa' trill before ascending and descending the scale with a staccato 'la, la, la!' After this concert, Willie uses her privileged position to smuggle out concentration camp footage but, in the meantime, Robert has been arrested and imprisoned. As a prisoner, Robert is subjected to psychological torture, forced to listen to the voice of his lover on a scratched record that endlessly repeats snatches of 'Lili Marleen'.

Willie's spectacular final Nazi concert occurs after she has attempted suicide, believing that Robert has been killed. The motivation for this show is the Nazis' attempt to disprove rumours that Willie has been killed by them; however, she has only agreed to appear on stage on condition that her lover will be set free. Once again the film intercuts her performance with devastating battle scenes. She is revealed at the Sports Palace in front of a huge swastika, in a long silver lamé dress and silver turban, her costume resembling a protective suit of armour.[50] Barely moving throughout her performance, clasping her hands stiffly in front of her body at her lower waist, she performs a fairly melodious *Sprechgesang* version of her celebrated song, accompanied by a female choir. In a sequence of shots that intercut between these images, her long-time pianist friend Taschner (Hark Bohm) is depicted dying at the battle front, listening to her. The scene finishes with a large close-up of her mask-like face staring directly at the camera and the audience, while a voiceover announces Germany's capitulation and the end of the war.

Before discussing the film's reception, it is worth commenting more specifically on Schygulla's vocal performance in these scenes. As an untrained singer (in her own words, 'not a singer but an actor who sings'[51]), Schygulla naturally possessed a decent voice within a mezzo-soprano vocal range. This was certainly good enough to meet the demands of a role depicting a competent singer, even though it could be unstable on certain notes. Despite clear differences of vocal range and timbre, Schygulla's intonation frequently invites comparison with Marlene Dietrich's inimitable and world-famous rendering of 'Lili Marleen'. Yet, overall, her performances of this song are uniquely her own and, for the most part, are used by the actor to establish her character's feelings and talent. What she stresses is the basic competency of her character. For Schygulla to repeatedly perform such a well-established song (one that had previously been interpreted by many different singers) with nothing more than adequate competency required a great deal of confidence in her own star power and image. To sing in a dilettantish or even bad way (e.g. out of key) would have been all too easy for the actress, as it would for any anti-star. On the other hand, it was far more daring to produce a rather mediocre version. Of course, French musicals like *Les Parapluies de Cherbourg* (1964) had already demonstrated that dilettantish singing could be very charming and also popular. However, *Lili Marleen* was no sentimental musical in the French tradition. At the very heart of this film was a troubling social reality, thereby undermining the claim made by numerous compromised stars of the Nazi period that their work was mere entertainment. Through Willie's repeated assertion that she is *only* singing a song, the film constructs her as a *Mitläufer*, someone who selfishly and uncritically conformed to the fascist political agenda.

The issue of mediocre talent achieving fame on account of Nazi patronage alone is made crystal clear in the scene where Taschner tells the singer that they have reached the height of stardom despite having no talent, while drunk and still deluded Willie narcissistically embraces her own reflection in the mirror, literally clinging on to her image. Within this context, Schygulla's stiff gestures while singing, along with her overextended, beaming smile and her forced tears, were highly appropriate, irrespective of the claims made by some critics at the time that her acting was wooden. Wooden was precisely what was required of her on this occasion. To achieve her performance, Schygulla undertook extensive preparation, including spending weeks watching Nazi entertainment films in order to replicate the vacuous emotional grammar characteristic of Ufa during the Third Reich. The sentimentality of these films is brilliantly captured in a coda where Willie meets Robert after the war for the last time. As she witnesses his triumph conducting a classical concert, a close-up reveals her with mouth agape, rendered dumbstruck in her admiration.

For *Lili Marleen*, Schygulla was required not just to play a star but, more crucially, a star lacking in talent. Stephen Lowry and Helmut Korte have suggested that Schygulla's typical acting style (which consisted of visible signs of performance) acquired a new quality in this film. For them, it was no longer perceived as a distancing strategy, as in the early films, but rather, through her diegetic star aura, Schygulla's playing of Willie produced an intensification of her actual star power.[52] Personally, I must admit some ambivalence about this idea of the film enhancing Schygulla's star persona, particularly as it received a very mixed reception among critics and reviewers in comparison to, say, *Maria Braun*. Thomas Elsaesser would later note that the film was too compromised for many commentators, especially foreign critics, who found its depiction of 'showbiz' as imbricated with the Nazi self-image too sardonic. He argues that it was 'Too sophisticated in its play with clichés and too twisted in its storyline for the general public.'[53] Furthermore, I presume, Schygulla's use of mere competence as a viable performance strategy for a star must have given Fassbinder a perverse satisfaction, since she had appointed him and he no longer liked her.[54]

There is no doubt that German critics were divided over *Lili Marleen*. While the tabloids took the film at face value, criticising the acting and use of clichés, the broadsheets recognised the explicit Sirkian play of clichés and double mode of address. Few reviews, however, discussed Schygulla's performance and, when it was mentioned, comparisons were unfavourably drawn with her triumphant role as Maria Braun. The respected film critic Wolfram Schütte commented on the role rather than her acting, stating that 'She remains the naïve German blondie … a long way from post-war Maria Braun.'[55] Other critics were more appreciative of the challenge, recognising that to imitate the facile glamour and demeanour of Nazi divas was of a different order than simply playing a historical character. Another critic praised (in a backhanded way) Schygulla's vocal performance: 'One knows that she can't sing, but that she does this expressively and powerfully, that is new.'[56] A more openly spiteful reviewer suggested that she was a 'moon-faced variation' on Marlene Dietrich, noting that the 'legendary song ... is sung quite ok, ... until her thin falsetto overdrive – Márléén; but with a swing more in the abdomen than in the voice'.[57] Other film critics commented that the interminable reprisal of the song on the cracked record effectively dissuaded audiences from ever wanting to hear 'Lili Marleen' again. Few acknowledged, however, that this had been the director's intention. As the film critic Peter Buchka commented, 'Like Robert, one can't bear to hear [this song] any longer. And this is indeed as it should be.'[58] In contrast, one critic even thought that Fassbinder had betrayed the founding ideology of New German Cinema and sold out to commercialism by reproducing

Granddad's Cinema in its sheer heinous ossification ... If Fassbinder had wanted to prove that he too can make the kind of cinema they as young filmmakers had once so bitterly opposed, then, awfully, he provided this evidence. The box office will be all right.[59]

The box office was indeed all right. An expensive national release involving the circulation of an unprecedented 150 prints,[60] along with a big-budget international publicity campaign, undoubtedly helped to make the film a commercial success. Schygulla dominated the posters for the movie, posing à la Dietrich/Lola before a swastika, thereby fully exploiting the Schygulla–Dietrich association. While Schygulla never thought of herself as the new Dietrich, it is clear that both the tabloids and a number of influential film critics certainly did. Andrew Sarris, although largely overlooking Schygulla's performance in order to focus on Fassbinder as auteur,

The Dietrich association

discussed *Lili Marleen* explicitly in terms of the director/star relationship of Von Sternberg and Dietrich, asking his readers to 'Imagine Josef von Sternberg and Marlene Dietrich in a recreation of the Nazi era instead of a foreshadowing of it.'[61] Vincent Canby's review was similarly auteurist, focusing on Fassbinder's perverse intention to turn a melodramatic sentimental story into a film 'as cold as ice'. Nevertheless, he did briefly note that 'Miss Schygulla is charming as the none-too talented Willie'.[62]

In the wake of *Maria Braun*'s success, the American film critics who tended to refer to *Lili Marleen* as part of Fassbinder's oeuvre granted little, if any, consideration to Schygulla's contribution. Similarly, the French reception focused mainly on Fassbinder's auteurist intentions.[63] It was in London, where the film was a major box-office success, that the press were most attentive to Schygulla, although their views were divided. While quite a few dismissed her singing as dreadful, Nigel Andrews marvelled at Schygulla's different vocal performances of the song that range from 'mischievous cynicism … [and] martial automatism … [to] drained and husky fatigue'.[64] Another reviewer attested to her 'Dietrich magic [because she does] not really sing it at all'.[65] However, a number of London critics claimed that *Lili Marleen* did the actress no favours, one reviewer even noting that the film displays her 'to cruel disadvantage, funny legs and all'.[66] Alan Brien, whose review started with a reprisal of his earlier *Maria Braun* eulogy, went on to express his disappointment with *Lili Marleen* and ended by stating that Schygulla was 'not without a certain bubbly cuteness with her moony smile … [yet she] acts with heavily signaled crudeness'.[67] Overall, the critical consensus appeared to be that the high expectations set up by *Maria Braun* were dashed by the use of clichés and nostalgic pastiche. Given the mixed reception, it would have seemed unlikely at this point that the film would become the springboard for Schygulla's future career as a successful cabaret singer in the mid-1990s.

In general, *Lili Marleen* reviewers often misunderstood Fassbinder's ideological conception of the film and, with it, the demands that this imposed on Schygulla's performance style. Broadly speaking, the film was a critical failure but a commercial success. It also kept Schygulla's international star persona in circulation, especially in the United States. Retrospectively, however, the German reviews can be seen as indicators of her waning national star power, which had begun earlier with *Berlin Alexanderplatz*. Christian Berger, writing in 1993, catches the revisionist tone of the *Lili Marleen* reviews when he states that

The same critics who wrote hymns of praise in the seventies, who acclaimed her somnambulistic aura and acclaimed her insufficient [acting] craft as promoting deliberate distancing effects, now discerned in Lili Marleen a 'lack of talent' and pigeonholed her as the 'most over-rated actress of film history'.[68]

He further notes that Schygulla's dispassionate response to such claims was that she merely considered the early praise of critics to have been as hyperbolic as their later criticism.

Conclusion

When the break-up between Schygulla and Fassbinder occurred again, neither thought that this one would be definitive or long-lasting. While still shooting *Lili Marleen*, Schygulla discovered that her leading man, Giancarlo Giannini, was being paid more than her, just as Löwitsch had been for his role in *Maria Braun*. When challenged about this, Fassbinder took it very badly. Nevertheless, Schygulla still assumed that she was going to star in his next FRG film, *Lola*, disclosing this prematurely in an interview in the American trade journal *Variety*.[69] This proved potentially embarrassing when it was later announced that Barbara Sukowa, Schygulla's former co-star, younger rival and rising talent, would be playing Lola. With this decision, an angry Svengali expelled his most celebrated star from his inner circle. However, the discovery two years later that Fassbinder's production notes for a planned Rosa Luxemburg film listed Schygulla's name as a possibility for the leading role suggested a tentative softening on his side towards the actor.[70] By this time, however, Fassbinder was dead, having died suddenly of an overdose on 10 June 1982, and therewith the possibility of reconciliation, of ever meeting and working again together, had gone for ever.

For many, the death of the maverick German auteur and trenchant critic of post-war West German society marked the end of New German Cinema. By the early 1980s, this branch of German cinema no longer had institutional and ideological support. Instead, state subsidies were directed towards international co-productions, giving rise to a more populist and genre-orientated cinema, and in the process a political drive and national distinctiveness were lost. With hindsight, both *Maria Braun* and *Lili Marleen* to some extent appear to have been transitional films, participating in this new trend, while remaining anchored in the former radical politics of 1970s New German Cinema.

To this day, more than thirty years after Fassbinder's death, Hanna Schygulla remains the star most associated with the director's oeuvre, despite all the other significant women who starred in his films. Surveying the range of roles she played in Fassbinder films, Schygulla once remarked that while the early parts as a 'backstreet Marilyn' were 'photographic negatives' of her own identity, the eponymous roles of *Effi Briest*, *Maria Braun* and *Lili Marleen* were her 'tragic sisters'.[71] More strikingly, she has linked these roles to her problematic relationship with Fassbinder, stating that 'The love story of *Lili Marleen* was our theme, so to speak, as it was in *Maria Braun*, which became our hit movie.'[72] Despite working with many other international auteurs, especially in the 1980s, her films with Fassbinder remain at the very core of Schygulla's star persona. This is a double-edged legacy. Due to this association, she continues to receive offers from international directors. Nevertheless, this has also both indelibly defined and fixed her star appeal for most of her audiences. Initially, she may have tried to erase his mark but, from the mid-1990s, she capitulated by cultivating the indissoluble bond between them. For instance, the potent figure of Fassbinder has become a source of continuous inspiration for her live cabaret act (see Chapter 4). Moreover, after relinquishing the prospect of a Hollywood career in the early 1980s, Schygulla appears to have been guided by Fassbinder's dictum 'to always courageously try out something new'.[73]

3 A TRANSNATIONAL EUROPEAN STAR IN SEARCH OF A POST-FASSBINDER PERSONA, 1981–9

In the early 1980s, Hanna Schygulla continued to develop her career as a transnational star from her base in Paris, where she had moved in 1981, mainly to be with the famous scriptwriter (and Luis Buñuel's collaborator) Jean-Claude Carrière.[1] The year 1983 marked a breakthrough for the actress when she not only won the prestigious Cannes Best Actress award for her role in Marco Ferreri's *The Story of Piera* but also regained her standing among North American critics with her performance in Andrzej Wajda's *A Love in Germany*.[2] Nevertheless, despite renewed critical enthusiasm in the United States, the attitude of the German critics hardened against her. Given the mixed response to Schygulla's international career at this point, it is illuminating to compare the reception of her two high-profile films in Germany and the USA.

'Europe's most exciting actress' or *un succès de scandale*?

Wajda calls her 'the most modern progressive and exciting actress of our time.' Ferreri sees her as 'magnetic, strong, powerful, a star who is a good actress.' ... Scola ... praises her 'comic touch ...'[3]

Just three years after finally parting company with Fassbinder, Schygulla confirmed her status as an international art-cinema star. She did so by appearing in a series of multinational co-productions, directed by eminent European auteurs alongside international stars. She acted with Bruno Ganz in Volker Schlöndorff's *Die Fälschung/Circle of Deceit* (1981), as the forcefully seductive Ariane, caught in the chaos of the Lebanese civil war of the early 1980s. In her first non-German film, Ettore Scola's *La Nuit de Varennes/The Night of Varennes* (1982), she played Countess Sophie de la Borde in a costume drama set at the outbreak of the French Revolution, enabling her to display her multilingual talent by delivering dialogue in fluent French. Schygulla was the German member of a prestigious international cast that included the French star Jean-Louis Barrault, the Italian Marcello Mastroianni and the American Harvey Keitel. Meanwhile, in Jean-Luc Godard's *Passion* (1982), she appeared alongside Michel Piccoli, Isabelle Huppert and Jerzy Radziwiłowicz, and in Carlos Saura's biopic *Antonieta* (1982), she played a contemporary Parisian journalist opposite Isabelle Adjani's passionate and fragile eponymous revolutionary. In Margarethe von Trotta's German feminist melodrama *Heller Wahn/Sheer Madness/Friends and Husbands* (1983), Schygulla played the liberated and intellectual Olga opposite Angela Winkler as the introverted Ruth. While this didactic feminist melodrama garnered few positive reviews around the world, in Germany Schygulla's performance received a considerable amount of negative criticism, the German critics making it all too clear that they had tired of her. At the height of the women's liberation movement, this film did nothing to endear her to the male critical establishment.

Having been keen to play more extreme roles since Fassbinder's death, Schygulla discovered her perfect project in *The Story of Piera* and her perfect collaborator in director Marco Ferreri, a radical anarchist with 'the talent of Fassbinder'.[4] The film, based on the memoirs of actor Piera Degli Esposti, is set in a post-war provincial seaside town in Italy. Its subject matter is incestuous and

The mother hopes for casual pickups in the
railway station while her daughter sits anxiously
at her side: with Bettina Grühn in *The Story of
Piera* (1983)

unbridled desire, one that drives a family to madness.[5] It depicts the
explicit oedipal desire of a father–daughter relationship, along with
an intensely physical love–hate relationship between mother and
daughter. While Piera was played by Isabelle Huppert, Schygulla was
cast as her mother, Eugenia, a restlessly roaming character, sexually
driven and guilt-free. Teetering between love and hate, Eugenia is
indulged by her weak husband (Marcello Mastroianni), a communist
intellectual who loses his job and the status that goes with it. Early in
the film, the precocious Lolita-like daughter (Bettina Grühn plays
the young Piera) observes and imitates her mother's sexual
encounters with strangers, trying but ultimately failing to protect her
from the social consequences of her actions, so that Eugenia is at

times subjected to electro-convulsive therapy to purge her of her compulsive libidinous behaviour. Eventually, the mother's unruly promiscuity culminates not only in her confinement in a psychiatric ward but also in the husband's disintegration in an asylum. In later life, however, Piera becomes a famous actor and, as such, is able to live out her uncompromising sexuality without fear of social sanctions, enjoying the sexual freedom desired but denied her mother. *The Story of Piera* ends with the reconciliation of the adult Piera and her mother, both of them naked and tenderly embracing on the beach against the pounding surf.

Ferreri's poetic film celebrates physical pleasures and their excesses through unabashed frontal male and female nudity. Schygulla, looking beautiful as Eugenia, as much as she did in Fassbinder's *Maria Braun*, is frequently depicted cruising around the town on her bicycle in search of men. Echoes of her Fassbinder films abound here as Eugenia tempts her potential lovers with the sight of her naked flesh, being repeatedly shown half-dressed in a carmine kimono over a black camisole, 'sluttishly' sitting with her legs nonchalantly parted. Unlike her German roles, however, this character is more energetic and sensual, as well as being dressed in more vividly coloured garments – notably, orange-reds. While her tousled blonde hair is short and softly feminine (often crowned with flowers), she is clothed sexily, even when cycling. Typically, she wears fishnet stockings, high-heeled shoes and a leopard-skin jacket over a tightly belted red dress. As this is not a social-realist melodrama, the real settings of grandiose fascist architecture and urban spaces appear devoid of ordinary inhabitants going about their mundane business. Consequently, areas such as the railway station and the beach acquire an abstract and surreal quality, the situations becoming quasi-mythical. This is particularly notable when Eugenia takes Piera to a Madonna shrine by the river to celebrate her first menstruation as a joyous rite of passage. Here, Piera suddenly notices a naked man bathing, emerging

Piera observes her mother's frank appreciation
of the guy's biceps

god-like out of a stream and inviting the young girl to caress him.
When mother and daughter embrace each other, the man lifts them
both up together, producing a symbolic figuration of pagan sensual
delight. This seems more like a utopian projection than a moment in
historical time and space.

With captivating grace and charm, Schygulla manages to
rescue her character Eugenia from the more sordid associations of
nymphomania that were prevalent around this time in films by male
directors. In Ferreri's feminist-scripted film, the sexually uninhibited
Eugenia operates as an archaic figure. Consistently on the move
(most notably, on her bicycle), she expresses above all else freedom
and sensual pleasure. Although Eugenia is an extreme character,
Schygulla's sympathetic portrayal and naturalistic performance evoke
an affectionate mother and loving wife. However promiscuous, she is

basically a likeable character, one whose appeal lies largely in her irrepressible zest for life.

An early scene depicts the teenage Piera in her quest to find her roaming mother, and the audience witnesses through the girl's eyes one of Eugenia's casual encounters when she is discovered joyfully dancing on the beach with a stranger. As the camera moves from long to medium shot, Eugenia is revealed pushing the guy down and straddling him, as she unzips his fly. This is intercut with a reaction shot (in close-up) of the daughter's intense stare, followed by a view of the mother (again in close-up) laughing, making wild-cat hissing and growling noises. As she lifts her head, Eugenia notices Piera approaching and sees her daughter smile. Eugenia's response is seen in close-up, as she makes an ambivalent gesture that first seems to beckon her forth but then shoos her away like an intruder, yet pleasantly, with a smile. In the final shot of the scene, the daughter reacts with a concerned expression.

As the adult Piera, Isabelle Huppert dominates the second half of the film, exploiting her reputation as both a risk-taker and a brilliant character actor who brings exceptional intensity to her screen roles. Here Huppert portrays a formidable theatre actress, one who both mirrors and acts out her mother's promiscuous sexuality. Huppert and Mastroianni are well matched here, noticeably so in their finely tuned interactions, such as the merely *suggestive* incest scene. In contrast, Huppert and Schygulla are typically revealed through direct physical interaction, such as embracing and kissing, rather than performing together in psychologically demanding scenes. This is possibly because Huppert's facility to exteriorise complex emotions through nuanced shifts of expression has the potential to jar with Schygulla's more stylised expressive manner. One of the few psychologically demanding scenes between the two actresses is a confrontation between Piera and Eugenia after Piera has 'freed' her from an abusive lover by seducing him herself. Here, Eugenia is sitting among

a group of men in the waiting room of the railway station as Piera arrives on her bicycle. Standing upright, she looks down on her mother, telling Eugenia that her own seduction of the lover was motivated to avenge her father rather than to liberate her mother, and that henceforth she will leave Eugenia to her own devices. At first Eugenia is pleased to see her daughter but then she suddenly becomes enraged, waving her hands emphatically. In this brief exchange, not only does Schygulla's pitch change abruptly when shifting from conversational tone to loud screaming but also her gestures appear too demonstrative, thereby contrasting with Huppert's more subtle performative shifts.[6] Tellingly, after this outburst, Huppert reacts with stillness, with just a faint intake of breath, before gesturing eloquently with her outstretched arms, waving and taking up an actorly pose, after which she leaves, telling her mother that she is resuming her acting career. Piera's action here, which simultaneously liberates and supplants her mother, arguably plays more to Huppert's strengths than to Schygulla's, who shifts too markedly between registers without tonal modulation. Consequently, this fails to evoke a convincing sense of Eugenia's volatile mood swing (motivated and justified by her impetuous nature). Instead, in this instance, it merely reveals the actor's lack of finesse when conveying highly charged emotions.

While the different acting skills of Huppert and Schygulla are exposed in this film, the two female stars do manage to depict the tactile interaction between mother and daughter with equal poise. In so doing, they provide a potent set of images that carry the film's feminist trajectory rather than simply encouraging erotic titillation. This can be seen in the final sequence, when Piera visits Eugenia in a psychiatric ward, the older woman depicted here as a lice-ridden vagabond in the process of having her grey hair shorn. In order to console her mother for the loss of her feminine glamour (and sexual appeal), Piera takes her back to the sea and the scene of so many amorous adventures. A shaven-headed Eugenia cowers on the beach,

sad and resigned, inhaling deeply. She then runs towards the ocean, discarding her clothes. This is intercut with a close-up of Piera smiling. Now, as the surf breaks in front of her feet, Eugenia waves her hands through the air shouting, 'Your father is here everywhere.' Then, in long shot with her back to the camera, she takes off her knickers and turns to expose the front of her naked body to the camera. Holding up her breasts, she declares, 'Look, you've robbed me of my milk, and now I haven't got any left!' In turn, Piera opens her jacket and responds with the question, 'Shall I give you mine?' As she exposes her own small breasts, they both laugh. Naked, Eugenia returns to Piera and tears her clothes off as though she were still a child. 'Down with all this useless stuff!', she says. 'Fly!' In extreme long shot, both completely naked, they tenderly embrace. In a medium-long shot, they kiss and, finally, the shot dissolves to the surf crashing about them.

     Unlike the earlier triadic configuration by the river, where the male agency of the pagan figure enabled (and participated in) the union of mother and daughter, this final dyadic sisterly embrace of adult daughter and mother has considerable resonance for a female spectator. More generally, the film's depiction of patriarchal society's attempts to control and pathologise Eugenia's unrepressed sexuality chimed strongly with debates in the women's liberation movement about the work of ideological state apparatuses like Medicine and the Law. The film's ideology implies that the mother's disruptive force, which leads to the destruction of the patriarchal family, is justified as a prerequisite for the daughter's liberation. Thus, the fearless Piera can be taken as a contemporary feminist icon, although only because of her mother's trail-blazing example of female emancipation. However, at the 1983 New York Film Festival press screening (which was the film's only US screening), Schygulla had to strongly defend the film's 'highly unorthodox view of motherhood'[7] to shocked audiences.

> I went into it knowing that the subject of incest was very touchy. But it was a role where for once, the character was speeding ahead of me. ... I need to be in films that say something and to play characters who really live out their feelings. That's when I feel I'm being stretched and challenged.[8]

As this statement indicates, the role of Eugenia clearly affirmed Schygulla's own sense of (feminist) selfhood. Moreover, it appeared to offer her a new radical screen persona, particularly when she announced that 'It's the first time that I can really identify with a role. She is a real rebel – a woman who thanks to her own conviction resists society, and despite social ostracism remains full of life.'[9] Later, in 1994, she commented that 'Ferreri's obsessive sexuality overcame taboos and thus forced me to go beyond my own imagined boundaries.'[10] When Ferreri died in 1997, Schygulla recalled that, apart from working with Fassbinder, this shoot was 'perhaps the happiest [one] of [my] entire career'.[11]

The Story of Piera's theatrical release in spring 1983 was limited to its production countries: namely, Italy, France and Germany.

In the States, loyal Schygulla fans appreciated her performance but took against the director. Vincent Canby was one of the few American critics who reviewed the film when it was shown non-theatrically at the New York Film Festival. He dismissed it as 'a lunatic cartoon', despite referring to the 'incomparable' Schygulla and declaring her to be 'as beautiful and mysterious as ever, even when the material seems simply to be muddled'.[12] In *Time* magazine, Richard Corliss recommended the film to 'only hard-core Schygullians', praising the 'fierce intelligence [which she] brings to every excess'.[13] Meanwhile, the British critic David Robinson, reporting from the Cannes Film Festival, dismissed the film as evidence of Ferreri's 'irresistible urge to scandalize'.[14]

Given the negativity of the American and British reviews towards the film and its director, it is perhaps not surprising that *The Story of Piera* was not released in these countries. In contrast, European reviewers were more sympathetic. The French reception was certainly more attuned to Ferreri's libertarian world view. For instance, Jacques Siclier discussed both female stars positively and commented on Schygulla's 'dazzling performance', her 'vitality and sensuality, like a capricious gypsy', while noting her 'fantastically regal manner' when she divests herself of youth and beauty.[15] Similarly, Bertrand Philbert considered her 'sublime' and a 'remarkable performer',[16] while *Le Nouvel Observateur* simply referred to 'la Schygulla'.[17]

Since Schygulla was the only German to win a prize at Cannes, the German reception proved to be generally positive about *their* prize-winning actress. As one critic remarked, although she appeared in Ferreri's film, 'this nevertheless also honoured German cinema. The prize is highly deserved. Never since Fassbinder's "Marriage of Maria Braun" has Schygulla been so good and nuanced, maybe one should even say: so wonderful.'[18] The renowned film historian Peter W. Jansen noted her quest for a new screen persona,[19] while the critic and film-maker H.-C. Blumenberg described how Schygulla's performance 'illuminates the ritualistic darkness'[20] with her searing sensuality, even though he found little to like about the film as a whole. In a similar vein, another reviewer praised her 'near painful intensity as the perfection of physical expression'.[21] Female critics, such as Sibylle Penkert, were at pains to elaborate the feminist dimension of the film, especially in relation to Schygulla's performance. Penkert considered how Schygulla had graduated from early roles that had 'instinctive emancipatory flair', via 'the intelligent female type' as in von Trotta's film, to finally personify 'the image of a woman in its excessive greatness' in Ferreri's movie. Penkert declared that 'It is *her* film.'[22] This feminist perspective, however, was not shared by one male critic who rubbished 'the dash of fashionable feminism' as simply a useful publicity tool.[23] The most dismissive review, though, appeared in the prestigious *Der Spiegel*:

Indeed she is fearless in attacking her role ... which is to say that she always fearlessly undresses, or is fearless when putting on her grey doggy-wig. And she always smiles softly, deranged ... She smiles ... her role to death.[24]

Schygulla herself remembered how *The Story of Piera*'s reception in Germany and France was heavily determined by national-cultural differences. Noting the contrasting interpretations when critics discussed Eugenia's proclivities and the incestuous family, she observed, 'In Germany she was a destructive woman who is responsible for what happens to the family. In France the film was understood as a love letter to life.'[25] Inevitably, the sensational nature of the film's utopian premises had some critics puzzled and others morally outraged. This, to some extent, explains its limited release and reception. The prestige of receiving the Cannes acting award, with its attendant international publicity, compensated to some extent for its nationally more selective distribution.[26] All in all, *The Story of Piera* was far more than a *succès de scandale*. In so far as it strengthened the persona of a sexually alluring woman of a certain age, it had a positive impact on Schygulla's career. Moreover, although very different, Schygulla's next film maintained and developed this star image.[27]

Opposing receptions

A Love in Germany was based on Rolf Hochhuth's famous 1978 novel, which in turn was based on an actual wartime event. The story centres on the themes of forbidden love and the madness of everyday fascism, set against the backdrop of village life in Germany during the Second World War. A middle-aged woman, Pauline Kropp (Hanna Schygulla), whose husband is in the army, falls passionately in lust and then love with a handsome and much younger Polish POW, Stani (Piotr Lysak), who is occasionally sent to assist her in the running of her green-grocery store. Pauline is so overwhelmed by her passion that the villagers cannot fail to notice. As a result, she is reported to the Nazi authorities for breaking the infamous racial purity law – the *Rassenschande* – through her adulterous sexual relations with a non-Aryan. Although a Nazi officer (Armin Mueller-Stahl) initially tries to save them, Stani is executed by hanging, while Pauline is condemned as 'the Pole's slut' and imprisoned in a labour camp. The film shifts between periods and style, with the wartime story being divided between Pauline's melodramatic love story and a bitter political satire about the sympathetic officer's attempts to negotiate the absurdities of Nazi laws and regulations.[28] These historical events are intercut and framed to go back to the present time (the early 1980s), as Pauline's son (Otto Sander) and her grandson return to the village to reveal the identity of the principal denouncer.

Although the Polish director Andrzej Wajda needed an interpreter to work with Schygulla, this did not prevent the German actor from receiving more guidance with her performance than with any of her other directors. Indeed, without his direction, she felt she would have underplayed highly dramatic scenes by performing them in a minor rather than major key.[29] Crucially, through the manner in which she developed a gestural repertoire for her character, Schygulla's playing of Pauline as a woman consumed by lust offers an opportunity for comparison with *The Story of Piera*. Throughout the film, Pauline inhabits a heightened state of passionate desire, usually looking quite plain in her navy-blue overall, often covering her face with her hands and repeatedly licking and biting her lips. At various times, she shudders uncontrollably, even beating her chest to stifle her own desire when she witnesses her neighbours making love.

There is one particularly furtive love scene in which Schygulla has to express a roller coaster of contrary emotions. This she performs in a manner of heightened naturalism, providing a very clear comparison with *The Story of Piera*.[30] Pauline is serving an older woman in the shop, when Stani arrives, forcing her to suppress her smile of pleasure. However, she cannot take her eyes off him and, as she continues to serve her customer, she tells Stani to retrieve something from behind the counter, giving him the chance to fondle her leg. As soon as they are alone, they embrace and move to the stairwell. Pauline unbuttons her blouse and, arching her body backwards and spreading her legs wide apart, she places her hand on her crotch, softly cooing 'Stani, Stani ...'. In the meantime, her little boy clambers down the stairs to surprise his mother. The lovers' sexual activities are largely obscured from the child's point of view by a door, the camera only permitting a glimpse of Pauline's enraptured smile. When Pauline catches sight of her son, her smile quickly fades, giving way to shock as she tries to conceal herself by closing the door. Then, reminiscent of Eugenia's actions in *The Story of Piera*, she simply waves to her child to go away.

Although in both *The Story of Piera* and *A Love in Germany*, the parental primal scene is observed by a child who is then waved away in a similar manner, each mother's reaction is played out differently.

Dangerous liaisons under the Third Reich:
with Piotr Lysak in *A Love in Germany* (1983)

Schygulla's performances in these two instances have to
accommodate the different conceptions that underpin each film.
While she had played Eugenia as an openly passionate and
promiscuous character, Schygulla portrays the equally passionate
Pauline as a woman who is much less self-assured. Unlike Eugenia,
who is guilt-free, Pauline is ashamed of her adultery, and this
transgression is further compounded because she knows that she is

also breaking the law of *Rassenschande* with a Pole. To express the ambiguity of a woman caught between desire and the law, Schygulla's performance suggests a body out of control and not quite in command of the gestures of passion. She does so with a series of uncontrollable shudders and twitches. Nevertheless, it is also worth noting that these movements are polysemic, being not only signs of passion but also responses to a range of social and personal situations. So, for example, she frequently puts her hands in front of her face to connote not only desire but also helplessness and shame. Similarly, her apparent involuntary shudders convey a range of emotions, including relief, reluctance, shock and shame.

A Love in Germany was premiered at the Venice International Film Festival in September 1983, where it met with an openly hostile reception from the German critics, along with a rather indifferent international response. To some extent, this was because the expectation was for something akin to the rousing political concerns of Wajda's recent production, *Danton* (1983). In this case, therefore, the reasons for the predominantly hostile West German reception were only partially related to Schygulla's performance. Arguably they also derived from Germany's fascist past and the attendant 'Polish Question'; more specifically, the Germans' belief that only they knew how best to negotiate, represent and come to terms with their recent history (i.e. the process of mastering the past, or *Vergangenheitsbewältigung*). It should be noted that Hochhuth's 1978 factual source novel had also been highly controversial, eventually leading to the resignation of a minister with a compromised fascist past.[31] It seems, therefore (explicitly for West German audiences and critics), that Wajda's film neither measured up to the complexities of the original novel nor to the director's reputation as a political auteur. Audiences and critics in Germany also resented a Polish director imposing his own nationalist perspective, especially by adding the contemporary framing story in which the now elderly inhabitants still deny that they played a part in the tragic outcome. As one annoyed German critic claimed, the film intended to demonstrate that Germans are 'still despicable'.[32] Wajda's own website is revealing in this respect:

[Hochhuth's book] gave me a chance to show on screen not only the collective past, but also the present of today's Germany. ... I didn't know the realities, and had to resort to fiction. The German audience sensed this unreality at once, which afforded them the opportunity to reject, with relief, the problems touched upon in the film. I'm not sure whether I wouldn't react in the same way to a film on a Polish subject made by Germans ... I could not afford to be generous and was unable to see the German point of view. As a result, even today I have the sensation that I had disemboweled my neighbour in defense of my own honour ...[33]

This same website also quotes Schlöndorff, who declared that even though usually he was no great admirer of Hochhuth, nonetheless, 'His book ... inspired Wajda to produce one of his most beautiful films. A film very uncomfortable for us Germans.'[34] His defence of Wajda contrasts with another quote more typical of the German reviews:

At the Venice Festival we Germans have a new reason to complain. Direction-wise, Wajda's film plunges below any acceptable level, the script is awkward, instead of some kind of lucid analysis of the special conditions of those Nazi days we get chaos and incompetence, and the actors, dear God, are poorly directed.[35]

The extent to which most German reviewers took pains to rationalise their rejection of the film is striking. Schygulla's performance especially was dismissed in highly purple prose, with one critic declaring that she seemed to be 'playing a solo show as if she was deserted by God, the world, and the director. With hungry eyes, lusty nostrils and hungry tongue she mimes a sexual person in need of intense medical care.'[36] Another suggested that Schygulla's character, with her 'continuous licking of lips, dressed in a slip, hands between her exposed thighs', was 'rather unintentionally funny and embarrassing'.[37] Others, though equally dismissive of the role, were more considerate regarding her ability, with one critic stating that the star was 'so dreadfully exalted that one would have to speak of the decline of a great actress were it not for her near simultaneous work with [Godard and Ferreri]'.[38] Schygulla's response was characteristically level-headed: 'It's the theme: which is a sore point for Germans.'[39] Regarding the damning comments about her, she added: 'I believe bit by bit they've become fed up with me.'[40]

There was, however, a marked difference when it came to her reviews by New York's leading critics, many of whom singled out Schygulla's performance as one of the finest elements of the film. In particular, her gestural repertoire, which had been so rubbished by most of the German critics, was widely celebrated in Manhattan as the culmination of Schygulla's star image as the alluring erotic woman. In a lengthy article entitled 'Hanna Schygulla Achieves Greatness', Vincent Canby, one of her greatest champions, acknowledged her risk-taking, noting that he had in the past been critical of the way directors such as Scola, Godard and Ferreri had failed to use her full talent. No such criticism was levelled at Wajda:

Miss Schygulla has at long last become one of the great European film actresses of our era [alongside Jeanne Moreau]. ... Though Fassbinder gave [her] a number of great roles, the role of Paulina is a once-in-a-career sort of part. ... The mysterious expressiveness that Fassbinder recognized in her ... has never been more amply realized than it is in 'A Love In Germany'.[41]

Fellow New York critic Richard Corliss concurred, stating that her performance 'dazzles with its emotional acuity', continuing:

Her gestures are pitched one stop up, perfectly in tune with the character's perilous rapture. Sexual heat sizzles through her body like lightning. ... It is a performance whose insolence and precision demand to be compared with those of the prima donnas of the silent screen.[42]

However, not all agreed. Some New York film reviewers even adopted the dismissive stance of their German colleagues. David Edelstein, for instance, described Schygulla's character as 'a basket case [who] jerks and slaps herself and nearly froths at the mouth with sexual desire'.[43] Though once an admirer, David Denby similarly failed to be impressed on this occasion, writing that she 'plays the role in the style of an unhinged Garbo: mouth open with lust, eyes popping'.[44] Thus, it would be an oversimplification to suggest that the New York reviewers were unanimous in their appreciation of Schygulla's work or that her New York reception was in all instances contrary to those of the German critics.

    A Love in Germany also met with a mixed reaction in Britain. Here, Alexander Walker, described himself as '[flinching] with embarrassment at Schygulla's eel-like eroticism', while others compared her performance unfavourably to that of Marie-Christine Barrault's portrayal of the malevolent, wanton neighbour.[45] The French reception was, on the whole, rather more balanced. In regard to Schygulla's performance, some were captivated by 'the extraordinary Hanna Schygulla',[46] referring to her 'ineffable grace', particularly in the way she 'inhabited the screen with all her blond subtleness'.[47] There were those, however, who criticised her acting for being 'too forced and too unnatural'.[48] Overall, it seems clear that the negative German reception informed the wider international reception of both the film and Schygulla's performance. Very few critics remained neutral when describing her idiosyncratic acting. However, such negative commentary proved less influential on the public, the film becoming popular with audiences, particularly in the USA where, as one German film critic suggested, people were fascinated by Schygulla's 'erotic motherliness combined with the lascivious melancholy engendered by the fear of the inevitable

Rassenschande judgment'.[49] The positive reviews and good box office in North America (although restricted largely to New York) were augmented by the film's success with the country's National Board of Review of Motion Pictures, which awarded it the prize for Top Foreign Film in 1984.

Waning star power and Hollywood: a promise not fulfilled

Throughout 1984 and 1985, Schygulla was interviewed and feted in the USA as a 'Screen Queen', appearing on the cover of *Vanity Fair* (January 1984) and hailed in Richard Corliss's 1985 cover story for *Time* magazine as the embodiment of the 'new European woman'. Here Corliss wrote that 'In each of these [most recent] films one can see the image of a new woman: standing proudly on the border of a social, political or sexual frontier.'[50] With hindsight, however, all this adulation marked the very tipping point of her star power. Her next film, Ferreri's *Il futoro è donna/The Future Is Woman* (1984), did not repeat the success of *The Story of Piera*, despite the fact that yet again Schygulla was cast as a sexually liberated woman opposite Ornella Muti. Not only was she disadvantaged by her co-star's youthful beauty but also the director's juxtaposition of her with images of Dietrich and Garbo backfired by diminishing Schygulla's screen image in the eyes of the reviewers.[51] As a result of these and other factors, the film was both a critical and commercial failure.[52]

Schygulla's first American role was as Catherine I, the future empress, in Marvin J. Chomsky's *Peter the Great* (1986), for which she commanded her highest fee to date. A big-budget television series that boasted a stellar cast led by Maximilian Schell, Omar Sharif and Vanessa Redgrave, this also brought her to the attention of a more mainstream audience. Although the domestic reach of the series might have led to a more prestigious Hollywood role,

Vanity Fair, January 1984, photo: Irving Penn/*Time Magazine*

Schygulla was surprised to be offered a supporting role in *The Delta Force/Mahatz Ha-Delta* (1986), Menahem Golan's airplane action drama starring Chuck Norris and Lee Marvin.[53] In the same year, she partnered Burt Lancaster in the television movie *Barnum,* as well as supporting Richard Chamberlain, Faye Dunaway, Sylvia Kristel and Ornella Muti in Simon Langton's international television co-production *Casanova* (1987). While none of these roles matched the high expectations Schygulla had expressed in interviews at the height of her fame, they certainly kept her afloat financially and maintained the circulation of her star image, providing regular opportunities for television, magazine and press interviews. Ironically, when David Lynch offered her the starring role in *Blue Velvet* (1986), she turned it down, thereby rejecting the one role that could have made her a Hollywood star. Her reason for doing so was because it reminded her too much of her earlier Fassbinder roles![54]

In her forties, Schygulla remained beautiful, her face remarkably unlined. She also continued to display her more mature and voluptuous body in the many different international roles she accepted during the mid- to late 1980s. However, during this phase of her career she was surviving rather than prospering, the films she made being largely undistinguished. Although American reviewers were indulgent about her comedic performance as a naively straight-laced German stranded in New York in the derivative comedy *Forever, Lulu* (1987), they were scathing about the film itself, denouncing Amos Kollek for his directorial ineptitude.[55] Meanwhile, many critics simply ignored Schygulla's role as a cabaret singer in Nazi-occupied Budapest in Pál Sándor's *Miss Arizona* (1988). Playing a vicious German governess in Cuba in the Spanish television film *El verano de la Señora Forbes/The Summer of Mrs Forbes* (1989) could hardly be seen as a highlight of her illustrious career, despite its script by Gabriel García Márquez. At best, it opened up much-needed opportunities for her in Spanish-speaking film, television and live performances. These became vital when, as an actor in her fifties, she was seldom offered roles in either American or European films.[56]

Conclusion

After Fassbinder's death, the end of Schygulla's career was anticipated by many German critics, a sentiment expressed in one negative review after another. For many years after his death she did not work again in Germany, admitting in 1988 that she had found the German criticism both hard to take and unjust. 'Nowadays,' she declared, 'whatever I do they demolish me.'[57] The German position is succinctly encapsulated by Christian Berger, who argued that Schygulla's style of acting, so perfect for Fassbinder roles, thereafter seemed limited and failed to convince in more naturalistic types of roles. In his view, her collaborations with Fassbinder had always been successful, even in the case of *Lili Marleen*, but as soon as she worked with other directors, such as von Trotta and Schlöndorff, her inherent weaknesses were exposed. Berger has written that 'Fassbinder having decided that Schygulla was his star knew how to work with her strength, her screen presence, but working with other directors her limited expressive range often worked against her.'[58] Similarly, Georg Seesslen has remarked that 'Every German film Hanna Schygulla made demanded comparison with a Fassbinder film.'[59] Such assessments of Schygulla's post-Fassbinder performances as innately limited have certainly not been restricted to German commentators. However, whereas in Germany they were widespread, elsewhere they tended to be less consensual and more individualistic. What I have outlined in this chapter has been a more nuanced assessment of her career development, while also accepting that some auteurs have been less interested in embracing Schygulla's specific talents than exploiting her existing iconic status as the inimitable Fassbinder star. Yet, while it is debatable whether Ferreri's and Wajda's utilisation of her persona was as compelling as Fassbinder's, they certainly did redirect aspects of it so that a new dynamic star image emerged. Had she been ten years younger, Schygulla's daringly unrepentant sexual persona could and probably would have gone on flourishing for much longer.

What is undeniable is that Schygulla's career output during the mid-1980s was astonishingly productive in terms of the range of distinguished directors she worked with, as well as the sheer diversity of roles she played during such a short period. Alongside other European stars, she benefited from broader institutional cinematic transformations, such as the accelerated growth of international co-productions (especially in Europe), which in turn enabled actors to shift more readily from starring in domestic productions to leading roles in European co-productions.[60] However, despite these changes, the notion of building a pan-European star system in the 1980s comparable to Hollywood was more aspiration than reality.

In Europe, the real stars were the directors. Even a decade later, Moira Mazzantini of Italy's The New Agency stated that 'they are the engines' who have 'the ability to attract the right producer'. Furthermore, she claimed that European film finances 'rely on good actors rather than star names'.[61] In Hollywood, star names are used as the main means of securing finance for film productions. The big stars are 'bankable' and are richly rewarded with high salaries and big-budget productions. Marlene Dietrich, Germany's most successful Hollywood star, epitomised Hollywood stardom of the studio era.

Although journalistic hyperbole had initially compared Schygulla to Marlene Dietrich at the height of her stardom (an association exploited in her films and foregrounded through publicity), the actor herself recognised that her independent star potential was far more limited than Dietrich's.[62] Schygulla's potential as a Hollywood star was inevitably limited, given that her fan base in the USA was largely restricted to New York. In this, she was typical of many continental European stars of the 1960s and 1970s: most notably, Romy Schneider, Maria Schell, Brigitte Bardot, Jeanne Moreau, Marcello Mastroianni and Alain Delon. However effusive the critical praise for a European actor's non-Hollywood performances, the parts she or he was subsequently offered in Hollywood were typically mundane, often starting with television roles as a means to test their Hollywood star potential. For most European stars, Hollywood has seldom been anything more than a career interlude. Hildegard Knef, for example, whose emblematic national status and international star trajectory prefigured aspects of Schygulla's career, arrived in Los Angeles in 1948 only to leave two years later without having played a single role. When she returned to LA in the early 1950s in a second bid for Hollywood success, she managed to secure just a few major roles.[63] For the likes of Knef and Schygulla, attitudes to female maturity also play a part in limiting their star potential once beyond a certain age. In addition to these factors, as Richard Corliss's eulogy to Schygulla implies, her persona and performance style would be incommensurable with Hollywood, given that 'US actresses are forced to work in miniature, to approach outsize feelings with the caution of accountants.'[64] While this is clearly a polemical oversimplification, it does lead one to speculate that Schygulla's star persona may well have been too problematic to be readily accommodated by mainstream Hollywood productions. An equally polemical claim would be that American audiences could more readily admire Schygulla's voracious sexual aura in foreign productions than in their own domestic films.

4 THE WILDERNESS YEARS AND HOMECOMING: DIVERSIFICATION, REINVENTION AND REAFFIRMATION, 1990–2012

When Hanna Schygulla reached her fiftieth birthday at the end of 1993, her film career was most definitely in decline. Ever resourceful, she not only branched out by working across various media, including television and theatre, but also reinvented herself as an international cabaret chanteuse. This strategy helped to keep her image in circulation, at the same time augmenting this image with her distinctive voice. In this way she remained busy, yet the parts she played did not maintain her glamorous image or lend her a coherent star persona. Indeed, she was not able to reaffirm her skills as an actor until 2007, when she created a deeply moving portrayal of a mother's grief in Fatih Akin's *The Edge of Heaven*. Now, at last, she emerged as an actor capable of embodying complex and psychologically rounded characters. This marked Schygulla's comeback. While not quite a phoenix arising from the ashes, she nevertheless reaffirmed that there was still genuine and untapped acting talent lying among the embers of her fading stardom. Even though subsequent roles failed to build on this new screen image, Schygulla had regained her footing as a distinguished transnational film actor. This transformation marks one of the most fascinating periods in the actor's career, providing the focus for this final chapter, which explores three interlocking strands of Schygulla's late career: namely, her roles in international cinema (notably her work with Amos Gitai); her tentative reconnection with German cinema via a new generation of directors; and, finally, her reinvention as an international cabaret artist.

Hollywood, European cinema and Amos Gitai

The prospect of a successful Hollywood career still beckoned for Schygulla at the start of the 1990s when leading British thespian-turned-film-maker Kenneth Branagh cast her in his film *Dead Again* (1991). Although a showcase for the director's own talent and the star potential of British actress Emma Thompson (to whom Branagh was married at the time), this Hollywood movie gave Schygulla the chance to reach a much wider and more mainstream audience, playing not one but two roles – an octogenarian and a dour middle-aged woman. For the former, Schygulla acquired layers of make-up to hide her still smooth, attractive features. At the time, she jokingly remarked that 'I never thought I would come to American movies as an 80-year old lady! ... I thought Hollywood was so glamorous.'[1] Ageing forty years, she plays a sinister German housekeeper with a past in a gothic psycho-thriller of reincarnated lovers. The verdict of Vincent Canby (one of her most stalwart New York champions) was that, although 'Ms Schygulla isn't on the screen long enough to call forth the personality of the woman who was virtually an icon', she nevertheless gave the film 'style and class'.[2] As far as reigniting her Hollywood career, however, this was another false start. Indeed, for Schygulla, Hollywood remained no more than a digression in her transnational career. Meanwhile, she continued to be in demand with European directors, who repeatedly (even though less regularly) sought to use her iconic image as a means to enhance their films. Throughout the 1990s, therefore, she played a variety of leading and supporting roles, most especially in international co-productions directed by newcomers.

Many actors, when experiencing a decline in their film career, accept roles in films by young and less well-known directors, particularly when the parts prove interesting or challenging by marking a departure from their more familiar roles. In this, Schygulla was no different. For example, in 1992 she accepted Polish director Janusz Kijowski's invitation to play a Jewish wife escaping from the Warsaw ghetto during the Second World War in *Warszawa: Année 5703/Warsaw: Year 5703*. In 1998, Schygulla appeared in a cameo role in Fernando Trueba's delightful Spanish satire *La niña de tus ojos/The Girl of Your Dreams*. In this star vehicle for the young Penélope Cruz, Schygulla produced a marvellously deadpan portrayal of the matronly Magda Goebbels, wife of the notorious Nazi Minister of Propaganda. However, in 1999, Schygulla's own inclinations were in a different auteurist league and direction, prompting her to approach the Hungarian Béla Tarr, who duly cast her in a non-glamorous supporting role in his bleak but visionary black-and-white *Werckmeister Harmonies* (2000). Years later, on meeting Aleksandr Sokurov, she expressed her desire to work with him, whereupon he created an outrageous cameo especially for her as a moneylender's demented and extravagantly clad wife in his film *Faust* (2011).

However, a more durable working relationship was initiated when Schygulla met the iconoclastic Israeli auteur Amos Gitai, having admired the formally and politically radical nature of his work. For many years, they would go on to collaborate on various screen and stage projects. The first of these was *Golem – L'Esprit de l'exil/Golem – The Spirit of Exile* (1992), stunningly shot by Henri Alekan. This parable about exile and the quest for a homeland juxtaposes a contemporary Parisian Jewish diasporic environment with the biblical story of Ruth. Alongside cameos by maverick directors (including Samuel Fuller, Philippe Garrel and Bernardo Bertolucci) and eminent theatre actors, Schygulla embodied the mythical Golem, the wandering spirit who was created to comfort those in exile.[3] At the beginning of the film, the Golem is created from the dust of the earth, emerging naked with somnambulistic movements, encrusted with the mud of creation. Throughout the film, Schygulla appears as a superimposed character, a guiding spirit in ever-changing guises that range from an expressionist figure to a contemporary Parisienne in a stylish black PVC outfit. More important than her physical appearance, however, is her mesmerising incantation of the Kabbala. Since the force of the spoken biblical and kabbalistic text holds the film together across the real contemporary and mythological settings, Gitai was particularly concerned to find a range of accented French speakers.

Interwoven with the overall musicality of *Golem*, Schygulla's distinct, slow intonation proves pitch perfect as she declaims the text in French by letting the words rhythmically flow on a regular beat and with little dynamic variation in cadence. Years later, in Gitai's film *Promised Land* (2004), Schygulla plays Hanna, a charismatic brothel madam. In this realist film that deals with the theme of illegal sex trafficking into Israel, Schygulla contributes a compelling cameo performance, soothing a terrified young woman who has been forced into prostitution.

Schygulla's regular collaboration with this maverick auteur has clearly been artistically stimulating for the actor in the latter stages of her career. Furthermore, Gitai's repeated casting of her in his productions recalls Schygulla's earlier and more significant role as Fassbinder's muse. For both of these highly politicised and formally innovative film-makers, she has clearly been able to embody and articulate their concerns. However, since these films were shown in festivals and retrospectives rather than being released theatrically, they were too marginal to have made a substantial impact on international audiences.

German cinema and Fatih Akin

In 1989 Schygulla accepted the starring role in Jörg Graser's critical *Heimat* film, *Abrahams Gold/Abraham's Gold* (1990).[4] This was her first German film after eight years of living and working abroad.

Schygulla adopted a broad Bavarian dialect for her role as a plumpish ageing hippy, the free-living Bärbel, who a decade earlier had left her infant daughter in the care of her despotic father while she travelled the world. Rather poignantly, Schygulla's character returns home to Germany to take stock of her life. For a film directed by a newcomer and released in the wake of German reunification, it received a considerable amount of domestic praise and was even made the official German entry in the Cannes Film Festival's Un Certain Regard category.[5] Interestingly, the German reviewers drew analogies between the fictional character and Schygulla's performance, which they read as both a homecoming and a return to the actor's Fassbinder persona. For example, Christian Berger, in his assessment of Schygulla's career, claimed that Graser was the first German director since Fassbinder to offer her a role that enabled her once more to embody a figure of unfettered freedom, stating that as 'a 1968 relic', she 'plays, of course, a part of herself'.[6] When promoting *Abraham's Gold*, Schygulla admitted to an interviewer that, despite all the reaction she had received in Germany, she would have still liked more offers of German roles, because she had a desire to speak her native language again and not to be, as she put it, 'Always the foreign body, the outsider.'[7]

However, the 1990s were not quite a homecoming for Schygulla. During the first part of the decade, she still appealed more to international directors than to the young and mostly commercially oriented German directors, many of whom specialised in lucrative 'romcoms'. It was not until ten years later, when German audiences had become bored with the formulaic qualities of such comedies, that a new generation of German film-makers rediscovered Schygulla. No longer in awe of her iconic status as Fassbinder's star, these directors seemed intent on having her in their films in order to invoke the deceased auteur's prestige. After 2000, Schygulla became something of a figurehead for the past epoch of film-making.[8] While this raised her profile once more, the consequence of this for

Schygulla, in my view, was that it effectively froze her image and made her film appearances seem both fragmented and gestural. At least in her work with Gitai she was always integral to the film, no matter how small her role might be. Given her astute self-awareness, it would be surprising if Schygulla was not conscious of this use of her screen image.

Between 2000 and 2010, her roles grew ever smaller in spite of her increasing cultural status. Thus, she featured more notably in the trailer for Till Franzen's low-budget debut *Die blaue Grenze/The Blue Border* (2005) than in the actual movie. Despite the fact that it opens with her voiceover, throughout most of the film she is heard more often than seen. Similarly, in Hans Steinbichler's much acclaimed and prize-winning *Winterreise/Winter Journey* (2006), Schygulla had little more than a cameo role despite the fact that she received top billing.[9] This meant that the actor's film work was confined largely at this time to undemanding roles that gave her few opportunities to demonstrate a maturing actor's talent. However, this situation changed dramatically when she met Fatih Akin, a prominent figure among a new generation of internationally renowned German directors. After his international success with *Gegen die Wand/Head-on* in 2004, Akin became Germany's most celebrated Turkish-German film-maker. He was, moreover, closely associated with a revitalised and vibrant popular 'dual culture cinema' that had previously only existed within the austere 'Minority and Migrant' strand of New German Cinema.[10]

Akin has explained that he was so 'enchanted' after meeting Schygulla that he created the challenging role of Susanne in *The Edge of Heaven* with her in mind.[11] At the core of this character is a former 1968 rebel who has grown into a disgruntled matronly mother; that is, until the random death of her daughter catapults her into unbearable grief. This German/Turkish/Italian co-production about generational conflict and border-crossing moves between Hamburg and Istanbul, intertwining the fates of six characters. In essence, it is

Schygulla, the character actor, with
Patrycia Ziolkowska

a melodrama filmed in a documentary-realist style, one that has a
deliberately over-schematic plot of cultural shifts and generational
rifts, along with explicit narrative parallelism, implausible coincidences
and chance encounters.[12] The film's schematic plot involves three
pairs of characters.[13] The first pair includes a German middle-class
mother, Susanne, and her student daughter, Lotte (Patrycia
Ziolkowska). The second pair features a Turkish prostitute, Yetel
(Nursel Köse), and her daughter, Ayten (Nurgül Yesilçay), a Kurdish
separatist activist. Finally, the third pairing comprises a retired Turkish
immigrant father, Ali (Tuncel Kurtiz), and his son, Nejat (Baki
Davrak), who is a German literature professor in Hamburg.

The first part of the film takes place in Hamburg, where Ali
installs Yetel in his house for sexual services and, after accidentally
killing her while drunk, he is imprisoned. In the second (interlocking
and overlapping) part, Ayten is befriended by idealist Lotte.
Ayten, who is on the run from the Turkish authorities, has come to
Hamburg in search of her mother. After meeting Ayten, Lotte offers
her protection in her mother's house. It is there that the two young

women fall in love. However, when Ayten is extradited to Turkey, Lotte follows her to Istanbul, where she is mugged and shot dead by a group of kids fooling around with the gun that she had recovered for her girlfriend. In the meantime, after disowning his father, Nejat attempts to make amends for his father's killing of Yetel by going to Istanbul to find Ayten. In the third part, a grief-stricken Susanne arrives in Istanbul and meets Nejat, who had rented a room to her daughter. She decides to take over the room so that she can mourn Lotte. Susanne eventually recovers by embracing the humanitarian political ideals of her daughter, ideals that had once been her own. Consequently, it is Schygulla's character Susanne who gathers together the various strands of the narrative and gives weight to the themes of guilt, atonement, redemption and the quest for identity. The film ends with Susanne forgiving Ayten, while Nejat drives to meet his father, who, having been deported from Germany, has returned to his home village in Turkey.

Susanne was Schygulla's triumphant comeback role, and this time she emerged less as a resilient star than a remarkable actor capable of producing psychologically rounded characterisations. This was an unforgettable performance. Most memorable is the sequence in which Schygulla's disillusioned and malcontent matron is both transformed and redeemed through an unbearable grief that finally unlocks the passion that once made this woman a rebel back in 1968. Up until this point, a bespectacled Schygulla has appeared as a dowdy figure, one whose life in the suburbs of Hamburg is devoid of excitement and passions. With the entry of Ayten into her life, however, excitement and chaos steal their way back into this orderly middle-class household. In one scene, as Susanne prepares a cherry tart at the kitchen table, the slow routine process of pitting cherry stones is disrupted by Ayten's 'Good morning' in English, to which Susanne grumpily replies in German, 'It's already afternoon!' The ensuing scene, which is semi-improvised in English,[14] plays off the placid Schygulla character against the animatedly gesturing

Beyond Fassbinder, playing the
malcontent matron

Yesilçay, as a political argument about Turkey's prospective
membership of European Union ensues. Provoked by Ayten's
comment, 'Fuck the EU,' the quietly spoken and passive Susanne
finally erupts, declaring, 'I don't want you to talk like this in my
house.' Once roused, Susanne becomes animated, raising her voice
and, holding the pitting implement against her cheek, she clasps and
unclasps her cherry-stained fingers while rebuking her guest.

As she shifts from deliberate lethargy to mounting anger,
Schygulla presents a portrait of an ageing and resigned woman whose
calm exterior is a facade for her disillusionment. She does so,
moreover, with just a few well-timed tiny gestures. This, however, is
merely the prelude to Schygulla's most dramatic and compelling
scene, one that lasts for just over two minutes of screen time. After a
grief-numbed Susanne has arrived in Istanbul and checked into her
hotel room, her pain unfolds through a montage of elliptical episodes,
lapses of time condensing the long, slow process of Susanne's release
of pent-up emotion, which gradually enables her to express her sense
of loss. At first mute and unresponsive, Susanne emerges slowly from a

trance-like state. After a lapse of time, she takes a mini-bottle out of the fridge, slowly unscrewing it and staring in front of her before throwing her head back to gulp it down. After another time-lapse, she pulls the luggage labels off her bags and unzips them, only to push them away from her before lying down on the bed and curling up into a foetal position. Then, following another lapse of time, the audience first hear Susanne before they see her. The silence and darkness of the room is pierced by a series of deep, throaty, inhaling groans that intensify into a sequence of drawn-out, strangulated, rasping sobs as Susanne's emotions can no longer be held in check. She erupts. Upright and keening, Schygulla pulls at the curtain, wildly flaying her arms around her, rocking, clawing at the carpet, beating the floor. Though barely visible in the low light of the room, she is dimly revealed by an elevated static camera. A further lapse of time brings the return of daylight, disclosing an open fridge door and numerous mini-bottles scattered about the floor. Susanne is sitting on an armchair making a phone call. She speaks in a calm voice as she introduces herself as Lotte's mother. A further time-lapse plunges the room back into darkness. Susanne is asleep, awkwardly stretched out on an armchair in a corner of the room. She wakes and is momentarily disoriented. After moving her head, she slowly gets up from the chair and opens the window to let in the noise from the street outside.

Akin's published script provides a simple directorial outline for the scene:

Susanne stands hyperventilating next to the hotel window looking at the Istanbul skyline, and then sits down on the bed bitterly crying. At dawn she has fallen asleep. At midday she dials a number on the hotel phone but without reply. Eventually she faints on the floor for a few hours. In the evening she gets up, greedily drinks a bottle of water, and then attempts another phone call.[15]

While allowing that Akin probably gave further instructions to Schygulla, it is clear from interviews that he encouraged improvisation and welcomed her input in developing this role. His DVD audio commentary explains how he set up the scene by installing a 24-hour CCTV camera high in one corner of a room to show most of it, including a window so that the changing light would indicate the passing hours through time-lapse photography. Schygulla was then left alone in the room with a full mini-bar (sufficient alcohol to divest her of any potential inhibition).

Schygulla's acting is a remarkable elaboration on the basic script outline, and perhaps only possible due to Akin's continuous recording of a '24 hour performance', which he subsequently compressed into a couple of minutes of raw grief. The intensity here is markedly different from her previous portrayals of bereavement (e.g. in *Maria Braun*).[16] This heartbreaking performance begins with the ordinary gestures of a weary traveller arriving and settling in to a hotel room. As such, it gives little, if any, warning of what is to follow, which is no less than a shocking aural attack: namely, Susanne's unrestrained howling expression of grief. At this point, Schygulla's acting approach is best described as lying somewhere between primal scream therapy and the traditional vocal lament of women who visit the families of the newly bereft in order to demonstratively express their sorrow.

It seems that Akin knew how to get the best out of Schygulla by working with her idiosyncratic lethargy, just as Fassbinder had, albeit through different means and using a different style of acting. Broadly speaking, Akin refrained from stylisation but instead anchored her physical sluggishness in character psychology by emphasising her fatigue from travel and grief when checking into the hotel room. According to Schygulla, Fassbinder forced his actors to stick exactly to his script in order to maintain his immense productivity. Akin, on the other hand, preferred his actors to 'deviate to find their character', having the luxury of a three-year production schedule.[17] The different naturalistic performance he elicited from Schygulla is highlighted when one compares Susanne's initial numbness and subsequent cathartic grief with the more stylised manner in which Maria Braun's expressive understatement of unrelieved grief turns into heightened numbness (see earlier analysis on pp. 41–3). This is not to suggest that she merely had to 'be' instead of 'doing'. Rather, Akin's approach facilitated for her something akin to Method acting, enabling her to immerse herself in the character and, at the same time, to remove any emotional blocks. As Schygulla would later admit, 'it was hard. Afterwards I was ill for three days, because I was so agitated.'[18] Thankfully, for Schygulla, her hard work and agitation were worth it. *The Edge of Heaven* won many national and international prizes,[19] with Schygulla being nominated for the prestigious German Filmband in Gold in 2007 and going on to win the American National Society of Film Critics award for Best Supporting Actress in 2009. The film's worldwide release met with an enthusiastic reception, many critics singling Schygulla out for effusive praise. In the States, the veteran critic Roger Ebert produced a review that eloquently captured the response of his generation to the film:

She was a young vixen once, then a sultry romantic lead and now she is a plumpish woman of 65. My own age … But what a woman of 65! Not a hint of plastic surgery. She wears every year as a badge of honor. And here she is so tactful, so warm, so quietly spoken, so glowing, that she all but possesses the film, and we love her for her years and her art.[20]

The British reception was also positive. Acknowledged as Fassbinder's former muse, Schygulla was praised for her performance in a role that ultimately 'binds and gives meaning to the fates of the others'.[21] For the French critics, Schygulla's actorly achievement of 'luminous generosity' transfigured her matronly appearance;[22] and in her role as Susanne, she was seen to bridge two decades of un-exportable domestic German cinema, taking audiences back to the cinephile films of the Fassbinder period.

In Germany, too, Fassbinder was used as a yardstick for assessing her now more naturalistic and deeply affective performance style. Daniel Kothenschulte, in the *Frankfurter Rundschau*, praised Schygulla for playing this maternal role 'with such toughness as Fassbinder could never have envisaged for her'.[23] Both implicitly and explicitly, Schygulla was acclaimed as 'the true event of the film',[24] in part because she surprised the critics with her unglamorous screen image and 'unSchygulla-like' performance.[25] When audiences had almost forgotten that she existed, Schygulla gave one of her best character performances and certainly one of her most moving.

'I'm not Lili. I'm not Marleen. I'm me.'[26]
Taking charge: the cabaret chanteuse

When, in her early fifties, Schygulla was confronted by a dearth of acceptable film roles, she diversified into theatre, including monologues and plays, as well as audio work, such as voiceovers for documentaries, vocal performances for CDs[27] and even audio-guides for exhibitions.[28] In 2009, she demonstrated even greater versatility by becoming a documentary film-maker with a film about (her friend) the Cuban actor Alicia Bustamente. Thereafter, she directed a number of short and experimental documentaries. However, perhaps one of the most significant outlets for her talents during this period was cabaret, which granted her greater autonomy than ever before, enabling her to conceive, control and perform her own stage shows. While this represented a new direction for Schygulla, it was actually a very well-established strategy, one previously adopted by a range of German female stars: most notably, Marlene Dietrich (on an international level) but also Hildegard Knef (on a more national level), as well as the former Fassbinder stars Ingrid Caven[29] and Barbara Sukowa.[30]

Schygulla's career as a chanteuse began in 1993, when the German/French television station ARTE invited her to perform some

songs for a programme based on the First World War. She further
tested the water by staging a couple of literary and song events in
Berlin, including the shows *Through Heaven and Hell with Faust* (1994)
and *Chansons* (1996).[31] Their success confirmed that the role of
cabaret chanteuse could provide Schygulla with a viable new career
and, in 1997, she developed her first major cabaret show, *Quel que soit
le songe/Whatever the Dream*, which premiered at the Avignon festival
in July. This French/German programme was based largely on
Fassbinder's work, and featured lyrics by Jean-Claude Carrière.
Although initially targeted at a French audience, it was subsequently
staged across Europe, as well as being recorded onto disc.[32]

Self-aware as always, Schygulla assured an interviewer in 1997
that 'Of course I know that for me originality is a better means to
impress than vocal gymnastics.'[33] Having acknowledged her status as
'not a singer but an actor who sings',[34] Schygulla has assumed the
role of 'diseuse', a subcategory of chanteuse that designates a form of
delivery that combines declamatory speech with singing. As early as
1996, while reviewing her performance in *Chansons*, Katja
Nicodemus described Schygulla's performance style as follows:

Hanna Schygulla has no great voice, but a nice full middle range which in the
higher register becomes breathy or disappears. Her expression is always a
quest for great pathos, the theatricality of the great diva. Eyes wide open, arms
spread out, expressive gestures. In her case it is difficult to say if less would
have been better. As [when working] with Fassbinder, on stage too she is at
ease with her mannerisms.[35]

That this quote captures Schygulla's signature style as chanteuse is
borne out by the few available YouTube amateur video clips of her
cabaret performances, as well as a documentary film showing her
performing in New York as part of the Museum of Modern Art's
1997 'Fassbinder Retrospective'.[36] Having been invited to this event
in her capacity as the ambassador for the Fassbinder Foundation,

Schygulla sings 'Rayon noir' (a string of Fassbinder's film titles embellished with witty one-liners) and 'Je suis le point d'intersection', a poem by the youthful Fassbinder that she adapted and translated. In her tightly choreographed show, these songs are framed by evocative reminiscences. When she makes her entrance on stage, the spotlight picks her out, revealing her hair (severely pulled back into a bun) and her long, stylish dress. Throughout the performance, she uses expansive and emphatic gestures to accentuate the lyrics, her chanteuse-style delivery segueing seamlessly between French and German, between natural speech and recitatives, between *Sprechgesang* and singing, and frequently between tempos and registers. For 'Rayon noir', she lets her girlish soprano voice vibrate before plunging into a Dietrich-style smoky mezzo, and here her dramatic pauses are particularly effective in masking her breathlessness. During her performance of 'Je suis le point d'intersection', she gestures demonstratively and literally. So, for example, when the lyrics refer to straight lines, she extends her arms, crossing them when she refers to a triangle intersection. In Laurence Kardish's appraisal of Schygulla's live performance at MoMA, he stated that it 'hypnotised' the audience. 'As in her films,' he observed, 'she sticks with simplicity and economy but with the expressive gestures and insistent modulation of a melancholic voice.'[37] Kardish also noted, however, that he missed 'The Schygulla Factor' and hoped that she would continue her film career.

Elle! Louise Brooks (2000–1) was another noteworthy event. In her homage to the captivating American silent film star who left an indelible mark on German cinema, Schygulla appeared and performed her own text (commentary and singing) to Roberto Tricarri's live musical orchestration, accompanying a projection of G. W. Pabst's silent film *Diary of a Lost Girl* (1929). Other international solo shows typically provided a mixture of literary recitation and musical arrangement, drawing eclectically on literary sources ranging from Bertolt Brecht to Jorge Luis Borges, and musically from Kurt Weill to

'Not a singer but an actor who sings':
Schygulla performing live at the Museum of
Modern Art in New York, 1997

Edith Piaf. These include *Kronos – Kairos* (1998), *Brecht … hier und jetzt* (2000–1), *Der Tango, Borges und ich – Hommage an Buenos Aires* (2002–3), *Traumprotokolle* (2002–3) and *Aus meinem Leben* (2010). Overall, the reviews for these later shows were fairly neutral. With many critics trying to be balanced in their praise and criticism, the reception spectrum ranged from claims that her 'unprofessionalism conferred a magic aura',[38] to dismissing her voice as a 'rusty squeezebox … [and the show] as a hammy medley'.[39] It seems that, like Kardish, some critics were missing 'The Schygulla Factor' associated with her screen image and were therefore disappointed because the show was 'a self-contained performance in character, rather than a projection of a stage persona that, one might imagine to be at least partly the performer's own'.[40] Moreover, since virtually all reviewers referred to her as Fassbinder's muse and international star, her singing career continued to be seen as a minor addition to her star image.

Conclusion

At the end of 1993, on the eve of Schygulla's fiftieth birthday, Christian Berger claimed in a widely read German newspaper that the actress 'nearly became a global star. Nearly.'[41] For many at this time, it no doubt seemed that the actress was unlikely to achieve greater levels of success in Hollywood or elsewhere and that, despite her many acclaimed roles, she would never attain the stardom of her great German predecessor, Marlene Dietrich. Such an impression was confirmed when Schygulla's film career fell into decline over the next ten years. Throughout much of this period (1994–2004) the actress had other priorities, including caring for her stroke-afflicted mother and her ailing father. However, 2005 marked another turning point in her career. Not only did New York's prestigious Museum of Modern Art honour her with a major retrospective but she also began to receive an increasing number of film offers. With *The Edge of Heaven* in 2007 she reaffirmed her acting ability and received a considerable amount of national and international acclaim. Finally, in 2010, the Berlin Film Festival gave her a 'Lifetime Achievement' award along with an Honorary Golden Bear, also paying tribute to her with a shiny brass star on the Berlin 'Boulevard of the Stars'. Henceforth, she would be lauded by some as one of Germany's greatest living film actresses and recognised by many as the greatest actress to emerge out of New German Cinema.

What is perhaps most interesting about Schygulla's career since 1993, apart from the sheer range of activities she has embarked upon, is that she has embraced her Fassbinder association and legacy much more wholeheartedly since gaining greater independence and control over her work as a performer. In her solo cabaret shows, such as *Quel que soit le songe*, she has paid overt homage to Fassbinder by incorporating some of his unpublished works into the programme. Similarly, his name has figured prominently in Schygulla's publicity and reviews as a reminder of her illustrious career. Thus, having tried to erase his mark during the 1980s in order to develop a new star persona, Schygulla has increasingly accepted and more actively promoted her Fassbinder-defined star persona since the mid-1990s. In Germany and elsewhere, Schygulla's star persona has been inextricably linked to Fassbinder, this being an opinion shared by her directors, critics *and* audiences. Since the mid-1990s, the actor has increasingly accepted the widely held view that Fassbinder was the director who, above all others, defined her career. After Fassbinder's long shadow had been cast across her career for over twenty years, Schygulla shrewdly brought him back into the limelight by incorporating his legacy to her advantage. As his former muse, she made his memory and his works a key instrument that 'played her tune'.

CONCLUSION

Any actor with a film career spanning several decades will inevitably experience a series of highs and lows, with peaks and falls in popularity and acclaim. Having experienced the joy and power of being in demand, many suffer the indignity and impotence of being out of favour. Few, if any, can maintain a steady climb to the top and remain there, unsurpassed indefinitely, unless a sudden death cuts them off in their prime, forever fixing their image and shrouding them in myth. Hanna Schygulla's film career was not only characterised by high and lows but also by a series of turning points and stepping stones, which she carefully negotiated with an insouciant confidence and intelligence. Through a combination of self-determination and serendipity, she built and maintained a long career with considerable resourcefulness and an indefatigable resolve to be, above all things, herself.

Back in 1985, the academic writer Sibylle Penkert made an astute and provocative observation in her pen portrait of Schygulla for the journal *Filmfaust*. Here she wrote that 'An actor has to let herself be made into something, very quickly, very acutely, and very present.' She immediately qualified this statement by adding, 'But she also has to make something out of herself, without anybody's help.'[1] With these two statements, Penkert nailed the dilemma facing film actors, particularly actresses: namely, how to relinquish control of their performances and image to someone more influential (e.g. a director, usually male) while retaining autonomy and, thereby, integrity and consistency. This is precisely the dilemma with which Schygulla has had to wrestle throughout her career. It is also one that she was, ultimately, able to resolve. Few actresses have managed to do so with such aplomb. Schygulla succeeded because she had something special, what Laurence Kardish (MoMA's former Senior Curator) referred to as 'The Schygulla Factor' in his tribute to her in 2005:

The viewer is always aware of her physical presence: her blue eyes, unmistakable face, enigmatic smile – both inviting and forbidding, and her simple, subtle gestures – a move of the wrist, a nod of the head, a crossing of legs – each of which is exclusive to the actress and yet expressive of the character.[2]

For Schygulla's admirers, such as Kardish, a crucial part of her star appeal has always been her inimitable screen image, one so striking that it produces a palpable sense of her physical presence. 'The Schygulla Factor has the audience believing at one and the same time in both the actress and in the roles she is inhabiting.'[3] Of course, Schygulla is not unique in her ability to make an audience simultaneously believe in the fictional character she is playing as well as being fully aware of the star playing a role. This is the essence of star acting. It is what star actors such as Bette Davis, Jeanne Moreau and Meryl Streep are celebrated for. However, in Schygulla's case, remaining identifiably 'Hanna Schygulla' was much more than a matter of star recognition. At the outset of her film career, she played a role either by citing other roles or by playing it as an extension of herself, and, in so doing, she suspended belief in the fictional character. In other words, the dilettantish and Brechtian presentational style of acting, which so clearly characterises her performance in *Love Is Colder than Death*, actually underpinned her rise to stardom rather than blocking it. In essence, it gave her a star-like aspect even before she was a star name or had a recognisable persona. It was only later, when she was *the* best-known star of New

German Cinema, that her idiosyncratic method of playing became a vital and explicit component of her character creation.

During the earlier part of her career, there was something unfinished about Schygulla's appearance. As Elfriede Jelinek, the Nobel Prize-winning Austrian playwright and novelist observed in 1990, this unfinished quality rendered the young Schygulla enigmatic but it also made her a blank screen (like 'a silk cloth thrown into the air') that could be projected onto.[4] Consequently, Schygulla was the perfect candidate to reflect the fantasies, desires and identities of her directors (chiefly, Fassbinder) and her audiences alike. What emerged around her at this time was a lascivious aura, one that would cling to her star persona for a considerable time, well into middle age in fact. As Schygulla herself noted, maintaining an effective star aura required her to both withhold and reveal, so that her private identity (as a person) inevitably gave way to an elusive star persona (her image). When interviewed by Sven Siedenberg for the prestigious *Süddeutsche Zeitung* in 1996, she admitted that 'Of course, one only shows a little part of oneself as otherwise one could not project onto me', seemingly aware of Jelinek's observation published six years earlier. Schygulla observed, 'Only in darkness can one project', adding, 'The actor has to some extent remain invisible.'[5] Yet, as detailed analysis of her performances in films as diverse as *The Marriage of Maria Braun*, *The Story of Piera* and *The Edge of Heaven* reveal, behind the relative blankness of her screen image can be discerned a series of crafted performances, performances possessing both precision and potency.

Having examined her career and performances in some detail, it is clear to me that Schygulla has extended her career well beyond expectation through a series of shrewd and intelligent choices. Such choices have enabled her to adapt her early sophisticated dilettantish performance style to a wider range of character roles, far more than anyone would have supposed possible. This is something that is seldom acknowledged even by her most ardent admirers, such as the New York critics. Of course, Schygulla has long been regarded as a star with cultural significance, exemplifying socio-cultural contradictions. Academic discussion of stars has often established direct links between various contradictions within a star's image and the social circumstances in which she or he circulated and gained popularity. As an embodiment of the zeitgeist, Schygulla has frequently been seen to represent a form of youthful anti-authoritarian rebellion and disillusionment associated with a generation of West Germans in the early 1970s. This is understandable given her formative period as Fassbinder's anti-star, particularly as he was widely regarded as one of the leading spokespeople for this generation. However, while Schygulla deserves to feature prominently in any assessment of the cultural significance of cinema in West Germany in the 1970s, this offers only a very partial account of her importance as a film star, particularly as she transcended her 'backstreet Marilyn' screen image towards the end of the 1970s.

Having become first a nationally acclaimed star (with *Effi Briest* in 1974) and then an international star (with *Maria Braun* in 1979), Schygulla certainly did acquire iconic status. As such, she can be seen to have embodied the historically changing values of German sensibilities, from imperialism through fascism to post-war reconstruction. With the passage of time, such roles might well have constrained her in terms of her image and diminished the scope of her work as a performer. However, by consistently working with prominent European directors in the early to mid-1980s, Schygulla avoided such a fate. On the contrary, she updated herself, coming to represent the persona of the contemporary sexually liberated European woman. Thereafter, from the mid-1990s, her work as a jobbing actor with mainly first-time directors undermined the consistency of her screen image due to a lack of sustained working associations and the sheer diversity of the roles she performed. This was exacerbated by her increasing involvement with various different media (theatre, television and cabaret), through which she maintained her public profile. While this might suggest that long-lasting stardom relies to a greater extent on having an identifiable and marketable image than consistently credible performances, clearly both factors are vital for a star's longevity. More recently, in the new millennium, Schygulla has assumed a more consistent public persona as one of the grand divas of German cinema. This has been due to a growing number of national and international Fassbinder retrospectives, in which Schygulla has participated, as well as a series of DVD reissues of his films. Thus, while Schygulla's rise to stardom was primarily dependent on Fassbinder, her longevity has also relied very significantly on her association with him.

The stress that has been consistently placed on Fassbinder's role in accounts of Schygulla's career is certainly warranted. No study of this actor would be complete or meaningful without such a consideration. However, this requires some degree of qualification if Schygulla's own part in her career is to be adequately acknowledged and better understood. For behind the myth of Schygulla as Fassbinder's muse/puppet lies the reality of a woman dedicated to developing not just a distinguished film career but as a human being through her work as an actor. Fassbinder, of course, casts a long shadow over the last five decades of German cinema. The danger of this is that it obscures the important contributions of his collaborators, including his leading female star. As this study has revealed, Schygulla has been much more than Fassbinder's prima donna. Having acquired this status, she moved on, yet still she remained haunted by his myth. In the 1980s, she tried (and seemingly failed) to liberate herself from her former Svengali's hold. Thereafter, she adopted a more pragmatic and entrepreneurial attitude and, having judiciously negotiated a series of short-term contracts with a wide range of international directors, she realised that not only was her own star image a significant part of her 'cultural capital' but that this also included Fassbinder's enduring reputation.[6] During her post-Fassbinder career, Schygulla delivered some very credible and affecting performances (even in some terrible films). She also turned her declining star power into an opportunity for a more actorly engagement with her roles (as did her contemporaries Julie Christie and Charlotte Rampling during the same period). While many ageing female stars of her generation retired and allowed themselves to be forgotten, Schygulla reaffirmed herself as an actor by repeatedly producing powerful demonstrations of her versatility and emotional intensity.

Schygulla, although the most beautiful of Fassbinder's striking divas, was neither *the* most beautiful nor the most versatile actor to emerge out of New German Cinema. These factors make her achievement all the more remarkable. For it remains an indisputable fact that Hanna Schygulla achieved a higher level of international success and visibility than any other actress associated with New German Cinema. In the process, she managed to sustain a powerful and provocative public profile, sometimes surviving but also prospering as a leading German film actor, enduring for much longer than anyone else who emerged from Fassbinder's inner circle. The secret of her success and longevity surely lies in her long-held determination to assert her agency and independence, boldly reaching out beyond the confines of Fassbinder and New German Cinema in a constant bid to set herself new challenges and experiences. Schygulla has refused to rest on her laurels. Having achieved accolades and won critical favour (most notably, in New York), she has continued to expand into new territories, test out new skills and try out new methods. She has persisted in the face of scornful criticism and indifference with what would appear to be an increasing sense of determination and self-direction. Possibly the very strength of Fassbinder's iconic image has forced her to venture beyond the kind of work she created with him in order to escape his shadow, arguably even forcing her to go to greater lengths in order to outshine him. Whatever has compelled her, the facts speak for themselves. Within and beyond the scope of Fassbinder's cinema, Hanna Schygulla has demonstrated a remarkable versatility, adaptability and determination to make her performances resonate with film-makers, critics and audiences around the world. Within and beyond the scope of German cinema, Schygulla has captured the imagination of successive generations, while refusing to allow her image to fix her indelibly as a nationally and historically specific cultural symbol.

NOTES

In virtually all cases, the key reference for newspaper and magazine reviews is the date of publication. I have also included page references where they are available. All translations from German and French source material, except where noted, are my own.

Introduction

1 See Sabrina Qiong Yu, *Jet Li – Chinese Masculinity and Transnational Film Stardom* (Edinburgh: Edinburgh University Press, 2012). She defines transnational stardom in the way stars 'physically transfer from one film industry to another' (p. 2). As distinct from international stardom, which refers to stars who become internationally famous thanks to films made in their own country (e.g. Fassbinder's *The Marriage of Maria Braun*), the transnational star is able to work in a different language than their own and make films outside their national film industry (e.g. Godard's *Passion* [1982]).

2 During the period of political upheavals and anti-Vietnam protests, The Living Theatre was at the height of its notoriety. Its confrontational and participatory performance style, itself based on the visceral nature of Antonin Artaud's Theatre of Cruelty, appealed to the radicalised youth and became highly influential for a new generation of theatre directors. For an illuminating and detailed discussion of these diverse influences on

the Action-Theater and anti-teater, see Jane Shattuc, *Television, Tabloids, and Tears – Fassbinder and Popular Culture* (Minneapolis and London: University of Minnesota Press, 1995), pp. 93–9.

3   Here I want to acknowledge the scholarly work of Stephen Lowry and Helmut Korte, whose chapter on 'Hanna Schygulla' helped me to start to identify some of the key issues I wanted to explore further: control over her own star image; diversity of critical reception; working beyond Fassbinder; and transnational stardom. Stephen Lowry and Helmut Korte, 'Hanna Schygulla – Der Star des Neuen Deutschen Films', in *Der Filmstar* (Stuttgart and Weimar: J. B. Metzler, 2000). A short essay by Sheila Johnston was also helpful. See 'Hanna Schygulla', in Hans-Michael Bock (ed.), *CineGraph – Lexikon zum deutschsprachigen Film* (Munich: Edition text+kritik, 1984).

4   Thomas Elsaesser, *New German Cinema – A History* (London: BFI/Macmillan Education, 1989).

1 Fassbinder's muse and anti-star, 1967–74

1   Fritz Rumler, 'Das Käthchen von Kattowitz, über die Schauspielerin Hanna Schygulla', *Der Spiegel* no. 51, 11 December 1972, p. 136.

2   Although the German term *Vorstadt* literally translates as 'suburban', which in English suggests a rather cosy sense of a middle- or lower-middle-class environment, it seems inappropriate for Fassbinder's depiction of post-war urban dreariness.

3   Johannes von Moltke is one of the few academics who discusses the lack of sustained research into Schygulla's star appeal in the dominant context of an auteurist approach. Von Moltke, 'Camping in the Art Closet: The Politics of Camp and Nation in German Film', *New German Critique* vol. 63, Autumn 1994, p. 93. See also Stephen Lowry and Helmut Korte, who acknowledge Schygulla's contribution to creating her star image. Lowry and Korte, 'Hanna Schygulla – Der Star des Neuen Deutschen Films', in *Der Filmstar* (Stuttgart and Weimar: J. B. Metzler, 2000), p. 220.

4 Hanna Schygulla interviewed by Edgar Reitz, in *Bilder in Bewegung: Essays, Gespräche zum Kino* (Reinbek: Rowohlt, 1995), p. 150.

5 It was not unusual for academic graduates and budding teachers to become actors, and quite a few of Fassbinder's inner circle had studied at university.

6 Rainer Werner Fassbinder, 'Hanna Schygulla – Not a Star, Just a Vulnerable Human Being Like the Rest of Us. Disorderly Thoughts about an Interesting Woman' (first published in German, 1981), in Michael Töteberg and Leo A. Lensing (eds), *The Anarchy of the Imagination – Interviews, Essays, Notes*, trans. Krishna Winston (Baltimore and London: Johns Hopkins University Press, 1992), p. 42. It should be noted that this lengthy 'critical appreciation' of Schygulla's development and contribution to Fassbinder's oeuvre was written in August 1981 after they had separated acrimoniously. She subsequently invited him to write his comments for her book: Hanna Schygulla, *Hanna Schygulla – Bilder aus Filmen von Rainer Werner Fassbinder* (Munich: Schirmer/Mosel, 1981).

7 Jane Shattuc refers to a 1967 Munich performance of *Antigone* by the American The Living Theatre. Shattuc, *Television, Tabloids, and Tears – Fassbinder and Popular Culture* (Minneapolis and London: University of Minnesota Press, 1995), p. 94.

8 Fassbinder, 'Hanna Schygulla – Not a Star', p. 204.

9 The Fassbinder Foundation DVD of *The Bitter Tears of Petra von Kant* (2006) includes Joachim von Mengershausen's documentary *Ende einer Kommune/End of the Commune* (1970), which features rehearsals, interviews and debates during the anti-teater period.

10 Schygulla, *Hanna Schygulla*, p. 29.

11 During this period she wore her own clothes and did her own make-up. Schygulla, *Hanna Schygulla*, p. 29.

12 For an extensive account, see Thomas Elsaesser's seminal *New German Cinema – A History* (London: BFI/Macmillan Education, 1989).

13 The title *Autor* for a film-maker was less the retrospective critical evaluation of 'auteur' and more a cultural label describing people working collaboratively and almost artisanally, like traditional artists,

and as such was intended to distinguish them from commercial and industrial directors.

14 As a national cinema, the New German Cinema was fostered as a 'high' art form, which in turn institutionalised the ideology of self-expression. See Elsaesser, *New German Cinema*, p. 44.

15 Elsaesser, citing Wolfram Schütte, in *New German Cinema*, p. 310.

16 Ibid., p. 285.

17 See Eric Rentschler, 'Director and Players', in Rentschler (ed.), *West German Filmmakers: Film – Vision and Voices* (New York and London: Holmes and Meier, 1988), pp. 167–8.

18 Thomas Elsaesser goes so far as to argue that without the actor as 'interface', the New German Cinema would merely amount to a collection of individual films or, at best, of its directors. See Elsaesser, *New German Cinema*, p. 286.

19 Ibid.

20 Thomas Elsaesser, 'A Cinema of Vicious Circles (and Afterword)', in Tony Rayns (ed.), *Fassbinder* (London: BFI, 1980; revised edition), p. 34.

21 Ibid.

22 Thomas Elsaesser, *Fassbinder's Germany – History, Identity, Subject* (Amsterdam: Amsterdam University Press, 1996), pp. 264–5.

23 Years later, Schygulla reprimanded herself, acknowledging that, unlike most actors who take a role as a role, she tended to consider it as complementary to her sense of self, as indeed 'an extension to her biography'. Retrospectively, she realised that playing roles as a means of self-realisation and self-knowledge could be seen as limiting her acting range. See Sibylle Penkert, 'Hanna Schygulla im Portrait – Von der Schwere und von der Leichtigkeit, ein Deutscher Weltstar zu sein', *Filmfaust* vol. 44, 1985, p. 8.

24 Fassbinder, 'Hanna Schygulla – Not a Star', p. 213.

25 Ibid., p. 214.

26 Ibid., pp. 205, 212–13.

27 See Schygulla, *Hanna Schygulla*, p. 29; and Harry Baer, '… had everything' [*sic*], in Juliane Lorenz (ed.), *Chaos as Usual – Conversations*

about *Rainer Werner Fassbinder*, trans. Christa Armstrong and Maria
Pelikan (New York and London: Applause, 1997), p. 54.

28 Penkert, 'Hanna Schygulla im Portrait', p. 9. See also Gertrud Koch,
'Die Frau vor der Kamera. Zur Rolle der Schauspielerin im
Autorenfilm – Frauen bei Fassbinder', *Frauen und Film* no. 35, October
1983, pp. 92–6, where the actors, including Schygulla, discuss their
work with Fassbinder.

29 Wolfgang Limmer, *Rainer Werner Fassbinder: Filmemacher* (Reinbek:
Spiegel/Rowohlt, 1981), p. 84.

30 Harry Baer (actor, producer and Fassbinder's close collaborator),
interview by Robert Fischer, is available as extra material on *The Bitter
Tears of Petra von Kant*, Fassbinder Foundation DVD.

31 Schygulla cited by Jim Emerson, 'Regarding Hanna', *Film Comment*
vol. 27 no. 4, July 1991, p. 74.

32 Penkert, 'Hanna Schygulla im Portrait', p. 6.

33 For a lengthy and nuanced discussion of Brecht's influence on New
German Cinema, see Shattuc, *Television, Tabloids, and Tears*, pp. 87–9.

34 See, for example, Ginette Vincendeau, *Stars and Stardom in French
Cinema* (London and New York: Continuum, 2000), p. 117.

35 See Andrew Klevan, *Film Performance – From Achievement to Appreciation*
(London: Wallflower Press, 2005), p. 5.

36 An adaptation of Fassbinder's own play.

37 Produced in 1970 but not released until 1992 when the music rights
were cleared.

38 While a traditional German *Heimatfilm* was associated with fascism (its
blood and soil ideology), New German directors critically deconstructed
its generic sentimentality of blissful rural living.

39 The director, Franz-Josef Spieker, was one of the underwriters of the
'Oberhausen Manifesto', premiered on 15 December 1969.

40 Schygulla received a joint award for her performance in this film and in
Fassbinder's *Whity*.

41 Joachim von Mengershausen, 'Karge Ballade von den armen Leuten',
Süddeutsche Zeitung, 7 April 1970.

42   R. W. Fassbinder, in Töteberg and Lensing (eds), *The Anarchy of the Imagination*, p. 6.

43   Thomas Wissmann (1997), cited by Lowry and Korte, 'Hanna Schygulla', p. 223.

44   James Naremore, *Acting in the Cinema* (Berkeley, LA, and London: University of California Press, 1988), pp. 80–2.

45   Ibid., pp. 28–30.

46   For Anglo-Saxon readers, this could be compared to the slight Scottish lilt of an Edinburgh voice.

47   Christian Berger, 'Die Abwesende. Hanna Schygulla: Vom Aufstieg, Fall und der möglichen Wiedergeburt, *Tagesspiegel*, 19 December 1993.

48   Günter Rohrbach, 'Geburtstag', in Lothar Schirmer (ed.), *Du … Augen wie Sterne – Das Hanna Schygulla Album* (Munich: Schirmer/Mosel, 1990), pp. 35–6.

49   Schygulla gained her first German Filmband in Gold award, although the film did not find a distributor until 1992. See Elsaesser, *Fassbinder's Germany*, p. 273.

50   In 1983, Schygulla described her initial distaste for *Petra von Kant*, stating that this was the first time she had made a film 'nearly with disdain', seeing herself as a 'remote-controlled doll'. See Koch, 'Die Frau vor der Kamera', p. 95.

51   Jörg Andrees Elten, 'Ich lasse mich nicht verheizen', *Stern*, no. 13, 22 March 1973, pp. 54–8, 157–8; and Harry Baer, *Schlafen kann ich wenn ich tot bin – Das atemlose Leben des Rainer Werner Fassbinder* (Cologne: Kiepenheuer & Witsch, 1982), p. 199. For more extensive accounts of the series and debate, see Shattuc, *Television, Tabloids, and Tears*, pp. 78–81; and Manuel Alvarado, 'Eight Hours Are not a Day (and Afterword)', in Rayns (ed.), *Fassbinder*, pp. 70–8.

52   Rumler, 'Das Käthchen', p. 136.

53   Ibid.

54   Ibid.

55   Koch, 'Die Frau vor der Kamera', p. 93. That Schygulla was acclaimed as an intelligent star is also clear from an interview in the influential left-wing

political German journal *Konkret*, where, alongside Fassbinder, she defended the progressive politics of the 'Workers' Series'. See 'Wer wirft den nächsten Stein?', *Konkret*, 3 May 1973, p. 19.

56 Effi's subsequent brief romantic liaison with a dashing officer, Crampas (Ulli Lommel), is only revealed years later, when the strict moral codes and conventions of Wilhelmine society lead to her ostracism. In the end, she cannot bear rejection by her estranged daughter and dies.

57 ursula reuter-christiansen, 'the abused effi briest', *Frauen und Film* no. 3, 1974, pp. 3–4; all original text in lower case.

58 Jill Forbes, 'Effi Briest', *Monthly Film Bulletin* vol. 45 no. 530, March 1978.

59 Peter Buchka, 'Effi Briest', *Süddeutsche Zeitung*, 6 June 1974.

60 Ibid.

61 Derek Elley, 'Effi Briest', *Films and Filming* no. 10, 1978, p. 42.

62 Mathes Rehder, 'Fassbinders "Effi Briest"', *Hamburger Abendblatt*, 17 August 1974.

63 L. M., 'Effi Briest', *Le Monde*, 17 June 1975.

64 Penkert, 'Hanna Schygulla im Portrait', pp. 7–8.

65 Fassbinder, 'Hanna Schygulla – Not a Star', p. 156.

66 Cited in Herbert Spaich, *Rainer Werner Fassbinder – Leben und Werk* (Weinheim: Beltz, 1992), pp. 349–50.

67 Hanna Schygulla, 'Ich will nicht länger seine Puppe sein', *Zeit Magazin*, 8 June 1973. Cited in Spaich, *Fassbinder*, pp. 349–50.

68 Cited in Spaich, *Fassbinder*, p. 52.

69 Cited by J. Hoberman in his lecture 'The Single Antidote to Thoughts of Suicide – Rainer Werner Fassbinder's American Friends', given on 10 June 2012, in Berlin, as part of 'The Hands on Fassbinder' programme of lectures and screenings. Available at: http://www.movingimage source.us/articles/authors/J.-Hoberman. Accessed 1 April 2013.

70 Cited by Robert Katz in relation to Schygulla's performance in *The Merchant of Four Seasons*, in Robert Katz and Peter Berling, *Love Is Colder than Death – The Life and Times of Rainer Werner Fassbinder* (London: Jonathan Cape, 1987), p. 77.

71 Baer, interview by Robert Fischer.

72 Limmer, *Rainer Werner Fassbinder*, p. 84.

73 Penkert, 'Hanna Schygulla im Portrait', pp. 7–8.

74 Rainer Werner Fassbinder, 'Kein Star nur ein schwacher Mensch wie wir alle (unordentliche Gedanken über eine Frau die interessiert)', in Schygulla, *Hanna Schygulla*, p. 187.

75 von Moltke, 'Camping in the Art Closet', p. 94.

2 From 'backstreet Marilyn' to new Marlene: the rise to international fame as a star directed by Fassbinder, 1975–82

1 Hanna Schygulla, 'Ein autobiographischer Text', in *Hanna Schygulla – Bilder aus Filmen von Rainer Werner Fassbinder* (Munich: Schirmer/Mosel, 1981), p. 31.

2 She believed at the time that she had not only given up on her career with Fassbinder but that she had also terminated her academic career when she abandoned writing her dissertation on 'Schizophrenia and Language in Karl Valentin'. Schygulla, 'Ein autobiographischer Text', pp. 32–4.

3 Hans-C. Blumenberg, 'Deutschlands tote Seelen', *Die Zeit* (n.d.). It was awarded the German Filmband in Gold for the ensemble actors in 1975.

4 Robert Katz and Peter Berling, *Love Is Colder than Death – The Life and Times of Rainer Werner Fassbinder* (London: Jonathan Cape, 1987), p. 126.

5 Günter Giesenfeld, 'Das Supermensch', *Deutsche Volkszeitung*, 17 May 1979.

6 He is also a producer.

7 Johannes von Moltke, 'Camping in the Art Closet: The Politics of Camp and Nation in German Film', *New German Critique* vol. 63, Autumn 1994, p. 97.

8 As, for instance, Lene in Helma Sanders-Brahms's *Deutschland bleiche Mutter/Germany Pale Mother* (1979) or Maria in Edgar Reitz's *Heimat* (1984).

9 von Moltke, 'Camping in the Art Closet', pp. 98–9.

10 Universum Film AG was the principal government-owned German film studio from 1917 to 1945 and became a major player in international cinema with its silent film exports. During the Third Reich, alongside its explicit propaganda films (which served most notably as vehicles for anti-Semitism), Ufa also made entertainment films (such as musicals, comedies and *Heimat* films) that only implicitly upheld Nazi ideals.

11 See, for example, Erica Carter, 'Sweeping up the Past: Gender and History in the Post-War German "Rubble Film"', as well as my chapter, 'Hildegard Knef: From Rubble Woman to Fallen Woman'; both in Ulrike Sieglohr (ed.), *Heroines without Heroes – Reconstructing National Identities in European Cinema, 1945–51* (London and New York: Cassell, 2000), pp. 113–27.

12 Sirk's melodramas are famous for his sophisticated use of irony, clichés, excessive pathos and his claustrophobic cinematography.

13 Thomas Elsaesser, *Fassbinder's Germany – History, Identity, Subject* (Amsterdam: Amsterdam University Press, 1996), p. 99.

14 Katz and Berling, *Love Is Colder than Death*, p. 138.

15 For a listing of awards, see http://www.imdb.com/title/tt0079095/awards.

16 Integrated promotion was then new for West Germany. See Anon, 'Man strömt wieder ins Kino', *Westfälisches Volksblatt*, 10 October 1979.

17 Inge Bongers, 'Die Ehe der Maria Braun', *Abend*, 17 April 1979.

18 Ponkie, 'Die Ehe der Maria Braun', *Allgemeine Zeitung*, 22 February 1979.

19 Hans-Dieter Tok, 'Grell, bissig, auch frivol', *Leipziger Volkszeitung*, 12–15 September 1981.

20 Nikolaus Marggraf, 'Liebe, Treue und Verrat', *Frankfurter Rundschau*, 22 January 1979.

21 Anon, 'Eine Welt der aufgeschobenen Gefühle', *Neue Züricher Zeitung*, 12 April 1979.

22 ge, 'Deutschland damals', *Südwest Presse*, 31 March 1979.

23 Giesenfeld, 'Das Supermensch'.

24 Horst Knietzsch, 'Melodram über den Tod menschlichen Gefühls', *Neues Deutschland*, 15 August 1981.

25 Stuart Byron, 'Breakthrough', *Village Voice*, 14 February 1980. See also Chris Sievenich, 'A Trailblazer', in Juliane Lorenz (ed.), *Chaos as Usual –*

Conversations about Rainer Werner Fassbinder, trans. Christa Armstrong and Maria Pelikan (New York and London: Applause, 1997), p. 230; Sievenich considered that Talbot's New Yorker Films and the New York Film Festival were the main sponsors of the New German Cinema and of Fassbinder's films in the USA.

26   Cited by J. Hoberman in his lecture 'The Single Antidote to Thoughts of Suicide – Rainer Werner Fassbinder's American Friends', given on 10 June 2012, in Berlin, as part of 'The Hands on Fassbinder' programme of lectures and screenings. Available at: http://www.movingimagesource.us/articles/authors/J.-Hoberman. Accessed 1 April 2013.

27   Similarly, Schygulla agreed to promote the film in London for DM 4,000 – as stated in correspondence, 13 June 1980, Filmschriftgutarchiv, Deutsche Kinemathek Museum für Film und Fernsehen, Berlin.

28   David Denby, 'The Marriage of Maria Braun', *New York Magazine*, 15 October 1979, p. 71.

29   Vincent Canby, 'The Marriage of Maria Braun', *New York Times*, 14 October 1979.

30   Judy Stone, 'The Marriage of Maria Braun', *San Francisco Chronicle*, 14 February 1979, p. 81.

31   Anon, 'The Marriage of Maria Braun', *Herald Examiner*, 18 November 1979.

32   Schygulla, in Dagmar Wittmer's television documentary *Deutsche Lebensläufe: Rainer Werner Fassbinder – Der Ratlose* (2005).

33   Cited by Byron, 'Breakthrough'.

34   Eric de Saint-Angel, 'Le Mariage de Maria Braun', *Le Matin*, 28 August 1980.

35   Gérard Courant, 'La Mort de Maria Braun', *Cinema* no. 254, February 1980, p. 80.

36   Jean-Philippe Domecq, 'Le Mariage de Maria Braun', *Positif* no. 228, 1980.

37   Jean de Baroncelli, 'Le Mariage de Maria Braun', *Le Monde*, 19 January 1980.

38   Michel Töteberg, 'A Market for Emotions: The Marriage of Maria Braun Production History', DVD Criterion essay. Available at:

http://www.criterion.com/current/posts/1047-a-market-for-emotions-the-marriage-of-maria-braunproduction-history. Posted 29 September 2003.

39 Alan Brien, 'Fassbinder's Brilliant Fairy-Tale', *Sunday Times*, 21 September 1980.

40 Anon, 'Hanna Schygulla, a Most-Sought Thesp, Mulls Future', *Variety*, 7 May 1980.

41 Sukowa had already previously appeared in a minor role in Fassbinder's *Frauen in New York/Women of New York* (1977).

42 See also Elsaesser, *Fassbinder's Germany*, p. 172.

43 Günter Rohrbach, 'Das Mysterium der Hanna Schygulla', in Lothar Schirmer (ed.), *Du ... Augen wie Sterne – Das Hanna Schygulla Album* (Munich: Schirmer/Mosel, 1990), p. 37.

44 It was West Germany's official foreign-language film submission at the 54th Academy Awards. The film failed to be nominated.

45 Manfred Purzer, who was then head of project funding, Filmförderungsanstalt.

46 Elsaesser, *Fassbinder's Germany*, p. 293.

47 The English version seems to have been rarely screened.

48 Fassbinder in Wolfgang Limmer, *Rainer Werner Fassbinder – Filmmacher* (Reinbek: Spiegel/Rowohlt, 1981), pp. 90–1.

49 The famous Lola pose adopted by Willie, but now in front of a huge swastika, is featured only on the posters (see p. 65).

50 Barbara Baum, the costume designer, explained that Fassbinder wanted exaggerated forms of costume. For this outfit he gave very specific instructions that it should resemble a protective suit of armor so that Willie could perform. Barbara Baum, 'Every Film a Challenge', in Lorenz (ed.), *Chaos as Usual*, pp. 156–7.

51 Cited by Ruth Valentini, 'Hanna's Metamorphosen', in Schirmer (ed.), *Du ... Augen*, p. 153.

52 Stephen Lowry and Helmut Korte, 'Hanna Schygulla – Der Star des Neuen Deutschen Films', in *Der Filmstar* (Stuttgart and Weimar: J. B. Metzler, 2000), p. 236.

53 Elsaesser, *Fassbinder's Germany*, p. 293.

54 In this sense, her approach was part of his general ploy to subvert the 'conservative' producer's cherished Lale Andersen biopic project.

55 Schütte also implied that she was not as accomplished as Barbara Sukowa playing Mieze (in *Berlin Alexanderplatz*). Wolfram Schütte, 'Verstimmtes Klavier', *Frankfurter Rundschau*, 17 January 1981.

56 Karena Niehoff, 'Deutschland, bleicher Vater', *Tagesspiegel*, 10 January 1981.

57 Ruprecht Skasa-Weiss, 'Grob, genial und gefährlich', *Stuttgarter Zeitung*, 16 January 1981.

58 Peter Buchka, 'Der Autorenfilm is tot! Es lebe der Autor!', *Süddeutsche Zeitung*, 15 January 1981.

59 Friedrich Luft, 'Opas Kintopp in Aspik', *Die Welt*, 16 January 1981.

60 R. W. Fassbinder on the *NDR Talkshow* (1980).

61 Andrew Sarris, 'Is History Merely an Old Movie?', *Village Voice*, 8–14 August 1981.

62 Vincent Canby, 'Film: Sweetheart of the Third Reich', *New York Times*, 10 July 1981.

63 *L'Avant-Scène* (no. 557, December 2006) devoted a whole issue to close analysis of the film.

64 Nigel Andrews, 'Lili Marleen', *Financial Times*, 19 June 1982, p. 5.

65 Anon, 'Lili, Lili, Rose and Rose', *Sunday Times Magazine*, 15 January 1982.

66 John Coleman, 'Lili Marleen', *New Statesman*, 15 January 1982.

67 Alan Brien, 'And a Nightingale Sang in the Alexanderplatz', *Sunday Times*, 10 January 1982.

68 Christian Berger, 'Die Abwesende. Hanna Schygulla: Vom Aufstieg, Fall und der möglichen Wiedergeburt', *Tagesspiegel*, 19 December 1993.

69 Cited in Katz and Berling, *Love Is Colder than Death*, p. 167.

70 See Juliane Lorenz, 'Eine Freundschaft mit Annährerungsschwierigkeiten', in Schirmer (ed.), *Du ... Augen*, p. 70. As it turned out, when the film was eventually made by Margarethe von Trotta, it was Barbara Sukowa who starred in *Rosa Luxemburg* (1986).

71 Gabriele Presber, *Die Kunst ist weiblich* (Munich: Drömer/Knaur, 1988), p. 21.

72 Juliane Lorenz, 'Hanna Schygulla', in Lorenz (ed.), *Chaos as Usual*, p. 14.

73 Hanna Schygulla, 'Kraft zum Widerspruch', in Schirmer (ed.), *Du ... Augen*, p. 68. Back in 1980, Schygulla's Hollywood prospects, bolstered by the critics and thanks to a sustained media exposure, seemed well within reach and, for a few years, she hovered on the brink, waiting for suitable roles. She was offered and turned down a key role in Marlon Brando's Nazi thriller *The Formula* (1980). She was also a prime contender to play the more challenging title role in Alan J. Pakula's *Sophie's Choice* (1982) until it was announced that Meryl Streep would play the part, for which she subsequently won an Academy Award.

3 A transnational European star in search of a post-Fassbinder persona, 1981–9

1 She had met Carrière while filming *Circle of Deceit*. Their long-lasting liaison was not openly discussed in the media until the 1990s, and then only in the briefest factual terms as they also worked together, not only scripting some of Schygulla's films but also writing material for her live cabaret and theatre performances.

2 Additionally, she was one of thirteen international stars to be awarded a special prize for her contribution to Cannes and the cinema.

3 Richard Corliss, 'The Passion of Hanna', *Time*, 4 March 1985, p. 40.

4 Kevin Thomas, *Los Angeles Times*, 18 December 1985.

5 The title invokes Pauline Reage's scandalous literary sexual memoir *The Story of O*.

6 I cannot comment on Huppert's vocal performance, as she is dubbed in the German and Italian version, and the French DVD is no longer available.

7 John Gruen, 'Hanna Schygulla Charts a Fresh Course', *New York Times*, 23 October 1983.

8 Ibid.

9 K. H., 'Amoralische Raubkatze', *Berliner Morgenpost*, 5 September 1983.

10 Ernst Schumacher, 'Ich wollte ja bewusst kein Star sein', *Berliner Zeitung*, 2 July 1994.

11 Frédéric Strauss, 'Entretien avec Hanna Schygulla', *Cahiers du Cinéma* no. 515, 1997, p. 33.

12 Vincent Canby, 'The Story of Piera: From Child to Actress', *New York Times*, 24 April 1983, p. 11.

13 Corliss, 'Passion of Hanna'.

14 David Robinson, 'Cannes Film Festival Irresistible Urge to Scandalize', *Time*, 16 May 1983, p. 7.

15 Jacques Siclier, 'L'Élément féminin', *Le Monde*, 15 May 1983.

16 Bertrand Philbert, 'L'Histoire de Piera', *Cinematograph* no. 90, 1983, p. 19. The journal devoted several pages to the film, including interviews with Fassbinder and Ferreri.

17 Marcelle Padovani, 'Les Folies ordinaires de Ferreri', *Le Nouvel Observateur*, pp. 65–6.

18 Florian Hopf, 'Goldene Palme für japanischen Film', *Stuttgarter Zeitung*, 20 May 1983.

19 Peter W. Jansen, 'Das Kino in Bewegung', *Tagesspiegel*, 14 May 1983.

20 See H.-C. Blumenberg, 'In der Fremde', *Die Zeit*, 27 May 1983, p. 35.

21 Anon, 'Lebensläufe der Liebe und der Sinnlichkeit', *Neue Züricher Zeitung*, 2 June 1983.

22 Sibylle Penkert, 'Die Geschichte der Piera', *Filmfaust* nos. 34–5, 1983, p. 31.

23 Hans-Dieter Seidel, 'Im Hitzestau der Gefühle', *Frankfurter Allgemeine Zeitung*, 10 June 1983.

24 Hellmuth Karasek, 'Der Welt die Brust bieten', *Der Spiegel*, 30 May 1983.

25 Sibylle Penkert, 'Unpublished interview with Hanna Schygulla', Paris, 10 November 1984, Filmschriftgutarchiv, Kinematek/Filmmuseum, Berlin.

26 It is also worth mentioning that although Ferreri was nominated for the Palme d'or at Cannes, he did not win it. They did make one more film together in 1984 (*The Future Is Woman*). Yet, as Schygulla wryly commented in 1993, because she, and not the director, won the major prize (as before with Fassbinder and *Maria Braun*), this probably foreclosed the possibility of a more sustained professional relationship. See Hanna Schygulla, 'Hauptrolle ist schliesslich Hauptrolle', in Lars-

Olav Beier and Gerhard Midding, *Teamwork in der Traumfabrik: Werkstattgespräche* (Berlin: Henschel, 1993), p. 183.

27   The poster for her next film, *A Love in Germany*, cashed in on her sexy persona, with Schygulla, shown reclining, wearing only a lacy slip and framed in semi-profile, facing Piotr Lysak with an enraptured smile.

28   Wajda added the framing story in order to comment on the historic present, where the former presiding Nazi officer was still living in the same village in 1983. He and Schygulla also interviewed the real surviving Pauline Kropp. Hanna Schygulla, 'Zu Andrzej Wajda', in Lothar Schirmer (ed.), *Du ... Augen wie Sterne – Das Hanna Schygulla Album* (Munich: Schirmer/Mosel, 1990), p. 96.

29   Ibid., pp. 94–5.

30   Later on in the scene, Schygulla was reunited with her former *Maria Braun* co-star Elisabeth Trissenaar (another Fassbinder star). The scene in *The Story of Piera* evokes a similar one from their earlier film together in which Maria's friend (Trissenaar) is in an emotional turmoil because she already knows about the apparent death of Maria's husband before the news is broken to his wife.

31   In 'the Filbinger affair', the conservative politician Hans Karl Filbinger had to resign after allegations about his role as a lawyer and judge during the Second World War.

32   Karena Niehoff, 'Ein lächerliches Lust- und Trauerspiel', *Tagesspiegel*, 28 November 1983.

33   http://www.wajda.pl/en/filmy/film26.html. Accessed 31 October 2012.

34   Volker Schlöndorff's statement for the French press, 1983.

35   Ruprecht Skasa-Weiss, *Stuttgarter Zeitung*, 10 October 1983. Cited on Wajda's website. Available at: http://www.wajda.pl/en/filmy/film26.html. Accessed 31 October 2012.

36   Dieter Strunz, 'Flickwerk der Gefühle', *Berliner Morgenpost*, 29 November 1983.

37   Beta, untitled, *Frankfurter Rundschau*, 4 November 1983.

38   Lina Schneider, 'Lehrstück über tödliche Gefühle', *Frankfurter Allgemeine Zeitung*, 24 November 1983.

39 Inge Bongers, 'Noch immer kein Meisterwerk, doch …', *Volksblatt*, 29 October 1983.

40 KZ, 'Die Liebe war ein Stück zu lang', *Bildzeitung*, 6 October 1983.

41 Vincent Canby, 'Hanna Schygulla Achieves Greatness', *New York Times*, 7 October 1984, p. 17.

42 Corliss, 'Passion of Hanna', p. 43.

43 David Edelstein, 'A Love in Germany', *Village Voice*, 20 November 1984, p. 58.

44 David Denby, untitled, *New York Magazine*, 10 December 1985, p. 95.

45 Alexander Walker, 'Hanna and Her Handyman', *Evening Standard*, 9 May 1985, pp. 22–3.

46 Dominique Jamet, 'Un Amour en Allemagne', *Le Quotitien de Paris*, 8 November 1983.

47 Christine de Montvalon, 'Un Amour en Allemagne', *Télérama*, 2 November 1983.

48 S. N., 'Un Amour en Allemagne', *Lutte ouvriere*, 12 November 1983.

49 Sibylle Penkert, 'Hanna Schygulla im Portrait – Von der Schwere und von der Leichtigkeit, ein Deutscher Weltstar zu sein', *Filmfaust* vol. 44, 1985, p. 10.

50 Corliss, 'Passion of Hanna', p. 40.

51 See, for example, Max Dildo, 'Mann oh Mann', *Frankfurter Rundschau*, 15 September 1984; and Inge Bongers, 'Ein Zukunftsbild voller Peinlichkeiten', *Volksblatt-Berlin*, 15 September 1984.

52 However, Ferreri's film was nominated for the Golden Lion at the Venice Film Festival in 1984.

53 John Stark, 'Europe's Incandescent Hanna Schygulla Blazes in Peter the Great', *People Magazine* vol. 25 no. 6, February 1986.

54 Graciously, she later admitted that Isabella Rossellini was perfect in the role and she might not have been as good.

55 The film pastiches the mystery quest of *Desperately Seeking Susan* (1985), with punk singer Debbie Harry's near-silent cameo as the titular Lulu substituting for Madonna's iconic role.

56 The 1992 television series *Me alquilo para soñar/I'm Available to Dream for You*, again scripted by García Márquez and shot in Havana, allowed

Schygulla to perfect her Spanish and thereby established her with Latin American audiences.

57 Colette Godard, 'Se protéger empêche d'avancer – recentre avec Hanna Schygulla', *Le Monde*, 25 November 1988.

58 Christian Berger, 'Die Abwesende. Hanna Schygulla: Vom Aufstieg, Fall und der möglichen Wiedergeburt', *Tagesspiegel*, 19 December 1993.

59 Georg Seesslen, 'Heilige Huren, Bleiche Mütter', *epd Film*, August 1991, p. 22.

60 See Blumenberg, 'In der Fremde', p. 35.

61 Cited in Mike Goodridge, 'Publicity: Star System Europe', in Marion Doring (ed.), *The Actor's Value: Does Europe Need a Star System?* (Berlin: European Film Academy, 1997), p. 7. See also Angus Finney, Chapter 4: 'Casting and Stars', in *The State of European Cinema – A Dose of Reality* (London: Cassell, 1996).

62 Marlene Dietrich's entire film-acting career spanned fifty years, and her cabaret and recording career continued until the mid-1970s.

63 She left again in 1952 to embark on a successful European film career, and subsequently revived her flagging career as a chanteuse. See, for example, Ulrike Sieglohr, 'Hildegard Knef: From Rubble Woman to Fallen Woman', in Sieglohr (ed.), *Heroines without Heroes – Reconstructing National Identities in European Cinema, 1945–51* (London and New York: Cassell, 2000), pp. 114–15.

64 Corliss, 'Passion of Hanna', p. 4.

4 The wilderness years and homecoming: diversification, reinvention and reaffirmation, 1990–2012

1 Schygulla cited in Jim Emerson, 'Regarding Hanna', *Film Comment* vol. 27 no. 4, July 1991, p. 72.

2 Vincent Canby, 'Branagh's "Dead Again", Homage to 40's Fiction', *New York Times*, 23 August 1991.

3   In a shorter version, *Birth of a Golem* (1991), the Golem emerging from the desert dunes into the glaring light was played by the singer Annie Lennox.

4   *Abraham's Gold* is based on a real incident and set in present-day rural Bavaria. It concerns the blistering post-war generational conflict rooted in unacknowledged Nazi atrocities and guilt, which continue to poison the present. Bärbel's father, a former concentration camp guard, recovers the hidden hoard of gold fillings extracted from the Holocaust victims.

5   Because of the centrality of the film's strong Bavarian dialect, its theatrical release was limited to German-speaking audiences, an inevitable limitation noted in an otherwise positive review by Kind [*sic*], 'Cannes Film Festival Official Selections', *Variety*, 16 May 1990.

6   Christian Berger, 'Die Abwesende. Hanna Schygulla: Vom Aufstieg, Fall und der möglichen Wiedergeburt, *Tagesspiegel*, 19 December 1993.

7   Thomas Thieringer, 'Ich bin ein Mensch, der nicht gerne kämpft', *Süddeutsche Zeitung*, 18 August 1992.

8   Hanns-Georg Rodek, 'Reue und Vergebung', *Die Welt*, 26 September 2007.

9   Josef Bierbichler was awarded the German Filmband in Gold as Best Lead Actor.

10 For a brief overview, see Deniz Göktürk, 'Beyond Paternalism: Turkish German Traffic in Cinema', in Tim Bergfelder, Erica Carter and Deniz Göktürk (eds), *The German Cinema Book* (London: BFI, 2002).

11 Akin, 'Interview' in the German press pack, Filmschriftgutarchiv, Deutsche Kinemathek Museum für Film und Fernsehen, Berlin.

12 In its use of coincidence, it makes an interesting comparison with Paul Haggis's *Crash* (2004).

13 Additionally, Akin extends and grounds the notion of overt parallelism in his choice of actors: whereas Schygulla was chosen as 'the grand dame of the German cinema' (as the iconic Fassbinder and New German Cinema star), Tuncel Kurtiz, playing a retired Turkish immigrant, connotes the early 1980s Kurdish cinema of the persecuted Turkish-born auteur Yilmaz Güney.

14 Akin's DVD auditory comment, *Auf der anderen Seite* (2008).

15 Fatih Akin, 'Auf der Anderen Seite' (Berlin: Deutsche Drehbücher/Deutsche Filmakademie e. V., 2008), pp. 110–11.

16 However, as in *Maria Braun*, when her back is turned to the camera, here too Schygulla portrays desolation not through facial expression (the CCTV camera is too far away for that) but through gestures and body stance.

17 Fatih Akin, 'Ich mag offene Enden', *Der Spiegel*, 24 September 2007, p. 159.

18 Schygulla, in an interview with André Müller, 'Ich habe Godard zum Weinen gebracht', *Frankfurter Allgemeine Sonntagszeitung*, 23 September 2007.

19 For the complete list of awards, see http://www.imdb.com/title/tt0880502/awards.

20 Roger Ebert, 'The Edge of Heaven', *Chicago Sunday Times*, 13 June 2008.

21 Jonathan Romney, 'The Edge of Heaven', *Independent on Sunday*, 24 February 2008, p. 60.

22 Quoted in Jean-Luc Douin, 'Le Theme de la reconciliation au coeur d'un maelstrom romanesque', *Le Monde*, 14 November 2007; see also T.S., 'Hamburg–Istanbul, allers et retours – Fatih Akin explore encore sa double culture', *Le Monde*, 25 May 2007.

23 Daniel Kothenschulte, 'Hinter der Wand', *Frankfurter Rundschau*, 27 September 2007.

24 Michael Althen, 'Doppelt tot hält besser', *Frankfurter Allgemeine Zeitung*, 24 May 2007.

25 Alexandra Stäheli, 'Liebe ist stäker als der Tod', *Neue Züricher Zeitung*, 4 October 2007.

26 This is the title of a *chanson* composed for Schygulla by Jacques Fransten and Jean-Marie Sénia.

27 Her performances include reading poetry for the popular *Rilke Projekt*, or for *Das Schmetterlingstal/The Butterfly Valley*, but also extracts from Sigmund Freud's *Das Unbewusste* (2006).

28 As for example, the 'Schwarze Romantik' exhibition at the Städel Museum, Frankfurt (2012).

29 Ingrid Caven, who has also lived in Paris since the late 1970s, has had a long and arguably more illustrious career as a chanteuse than as an actor.

30 Barbara Sukowa specialises in performing dramatic *Sprechgesang* in Schönberg's work and other classical music.

31 In Germany, this is a common theatrical genre.

32 Hanna Schygulla, *Chantsingt* (Erato Disques, 1997).

33 Helmut Mauro, 'Der neue Spatz von Avignon', *Süddeutsche Zeitung*, 2 October 1997.

34 Ruth Valentini, 'Hanna's Metamorphosen', in Lothar Schirmer (ed.), *Du … Augen wie Sterne – Das Hanna Schygulla Album* (Munich: Schirmer/Mosel, 1990), p. 153.

35 Katja Nicodemus, 'Madonnenhaft: Hanna Schygulla singt', *Tageszeitung*, 11 September 1996.

36 Juliane Lorenz's 1997 Fassbinder documentary *Life, Love and Celluloid*, about his US reception and the New German Cinema, is available as extra material on *The Merchant of Four Seasons*, Fassbinder Foundation DVD (2006).

37 Laurence Kardish, 'In den hypnotisierten Augen Amerikas', in Schirmer (ed.), *Du … Augen wie Sterne*, p. 32.

38 Manuel Brug, 'Mamma, das Messer', *Tagesspiegel*, 11 September 1996.

39 A. J. Goldmann, 'Schygulla Sings!', *New York Feuilleton*, 10 June 2005.

40 Adam Sweeting, 'Hanna Schygulla', *Guardian*, 21 June 2000.

41 Berger, 'Die Abwesende'.

Conclusion

1 Sibylle Penkert, 'Hanna Schygulla im Portrait – Von der Schwere und von der Leichtigkeit, ein Deutscher Weltstar zu sein', *Filmfaust* vol. 44, 1985, p. 9.

2 Laurence Kardish, 'Tribute to Hanna Schygulla at MoMA, New York', 6 September 2005. Available at: http://rwff.org/node.php/en/news_detail/47. Accessed 3 November 2010.

3 Ibid.

4 Elfriede Jelinek, 'Kein verworfenes Gesicht', in Lothar Schirmer (ed.),
Du ... Augen wie Sterne – Das Hanna Schygulla Album (Munich:
Schirmer/Mosel, 1990), p. 25.

5 Interview with Sven Siedenberg, 'Manchmal quäle ich mich auch',
Süddeutsche Zeitung, 11 July 1996.

6 Until 1994, the German state functioned as a casting agency monopoly,
which meant that no private individual or enterprise was allowed to work
as an agent for actors. See Malte Hagener, 'German Stars of the 1990s',
in Tim Bergfelder, Erica Carter and Deniz Göktürk (eds), *The German
Cinema Book* (London: BFI, 2002), p. 100.

BIBLIOGRAPHY

Included here are books, chapters and articles consulted for this work and cited, along with a selection of further reading. Reviews and interviews from periodicals and general journals are cited in the endnotes for each chapter.

Alberich, Enrique, 'Interview with Carlos Saura', in Linda M. Willem (ed.), *Carlos Saura* (Jackson: University of Mississippi Press, 2003), pp. 65–71.

Alvarado, Manuel, 'Eight Hours Are not a Day (and Afterword)', in Tony Rayns (ed.), *Fassbinder* (London: BFI, 1980; revised edition), pp. 70–8.

Baer, Harry, *Schlafen kann ich wenn ich tot bin: Das atemlose Leben des Rainer Werner Fassbinder* (Cologne: Kiepenheuer & Witsch, 1982).

Baer, Harry, '… had everything', in Lorenz (ed.), *Chaos as Usual*, pp. 47–60.

Baum, Barbara, 'Every Film a Challenge', in Lorenz (ed.), *Chaos as Usual*, pp. 153–60.

Bensoussan, Georges, 'Entretien avec Hanna Schygulla – Star ou pas?', *Cahiers du Cinéma* vol. 322 no. 14, April 1981, pp. iii–iv.

Berger, Tim, 'German Actors in Hollywood: The Long View', in Phillips and Vincendeau (eds), *Journeys of Desire*, pp. 37–43.

Carter, Erica, 'Sweeping up the Past: Gender and History in the Post-War German "Rubble Film"', in Ulrike Sieglohr (ed.), *Heroines without Heroes: Reconstructing National Identities in European Cinema, 1945–51* (London and New York: Cassell, 2000), pp. 91–111.

Corliss, Richard, 'The Passion of Hanna', *Time*, 4 March 1985, pp. 40–5.

Courant, Gérard, 'La Mort de Maria Braun', *Cinema* no. 254, February 1980, pp. 78–81.

Domecq, Jean-Philippe, 'Le Mariage de Maria Braun', *Positif* no. 228, 1980, pp. 65–6.

Dyer, Richard, *Stars* (London: BFI, 1979).

Elley, Derek, 'Effi Briest', *Films and Filming* no. 10, 1978, p. 42.

Elsaesser, Thomas, 'A Cinema of Vicious Circles (and Afterword)', in Tony Rayns (ed.), *Fassbinder* (London: BFI, 1980; revised edition), pp. 24–53.

Elsaesser, Thomas, *New German Cinema: A History* (London: BFI/Macmillan Education, 1989).

Elsaesser, Thomas, *Fassbinder's Germany: History, Identity, Subject* (Amsterdam: Amsterdam University Press, 1996).

Elsaesser, Thomas and Michael Wedel (eds), *The BFI Companion to German Cinema* (London: BFI/Cassell, 1999).

Emerson, Jim, 'Regarding Hanna', *Film Comment* vol. 27 no. 4, July 1991, pp. 72–4.

Fassbinder, Rainer Werner, 'Kein Star nur ein schwacher Mensch wie wir alle (unordentliche Gedanken über eine Frau die interessiert)', in Schygulla, *Hanna Schygulla*, pp. 168–87.

Fassbinder, Rainer Werner, 'Hanna Schygulla: Not a Star, Just a Vulnerable Human Being Like the Rest of Us. Disorderly Thoughts about an Interesting Woman' (first published in German, 1981), in Töteberg and Lensing (eds), *The Anarchy of the Imagination*, pp. 199–214.

Finney, Angus, Chapter 4: 'Casting and Stars', in *The State of European Cinema: A Dose of Reality* (London: Cassell, 1996), pp. 52–66.

Fisher, William, 'Eat Europudding', *Sight and Sound* no. 59, Autumn 1990, pp. 224–7.

Forbes, Jill, 'Effi Briest', *Monthly Film Bulletin* vol. 45 no. 530, March 1978, pp. 45–6.

Geraghty, Christine, 'Re-examining Stardom: Questions of Texts, Bodies and Performance', in Christine Gledhill and Linda Williams (eds), *Reinventing Film Studies* (London: Arnold, 2000), pp. 183–201.

Gledhill, Christine (ed.), *Stardom: Industry of Desire* (London: Routledge, 1991).

Göktürk, Deniz, 'Beyond Paternalism: Turkish German Traffic in Cinema', in Tim Bergfelder, Erica Carter and Deniz Göktürk (eds), *The German Cinema Book* (London: BFI, 2002), pp. 248–55.

Goodridge, Mike, 'Publicity: Star System Europe', in Marion Doring (ed.), *The Actor's Value: Does Europe Need a Star System?* (Berlin: European Film Academy, 1997), pp. 8–20.

Hagener, Malte, 'German Stars of the 1990s', in Tim Bergfelder, Erica Carter and Deniz Göktürk (eds), *The German Cinema Book* (London: BFI, 2002), pp. 98–105.

Hayman, Ronald, *Fassbinder: Film Maker* (London: Weidenfeld & Nicolson, 1984).

Jelinek, Elfriede, 'Kein verworfenes Gesicht', in Schirmer (ed.), *Du ... Augen wie Sterne*, pp. 25–8.

Johnston, Sheila, 'Hanna Schygulla', in Hans-Michael Bock (ed.), *CineGraph: Lexikon zum deutschsprachigen Film* (Munich: Edition text+kritik, 1984), unpaginated.

Kardish, Laurence, 'In den hypnotisierten Augen Amerikas', in Schirmer (ed.), *Du ... Augen wie Sterne*, pp. 31–2.

Katz, Robert and Peter Berling, *Love Is Colder than Death: The Life and Times of Rainer Werner Fassbinder* (London: Jonathan Cape, 1987).

Klevan, Andrew, *Film Performance: From Achievement to Appreciation* (London: Wallflower Press, 2005).

Koch, Gertrud, 'Die Frau vor der Kamera. Zur Rolle der Schauspielerin im Autorenfilm: Frauen bei Fassbinder', *Frauen und Film* no. 35, October 1983, pp. 92–6.

Limmer, Wolfgang, *Rainer Werner Fassbinder: Filmmacher* (Reinbek: Spiegel/Rowohlt, 1981).

Lorenz, Juliane, 'Eine Freundschaft mit Annährerungsschwierigkeiten', in Schirmer (ed.), *Du ... Augen wie Sterne*, pp. 69–70.

Lorenz, Juliane (ed.), *Chaos as Usual: Conversations about Rainer Werner Fassbinder*, trans. Christa Armstrong and Maria Pelikan (New York and London: Applause, 1997).

Lowry, Stephen and Helmut Korte, *Der Filmstar* (Stuttgart and Weimar: J. B. Metzler, 2000).

Lowry, Stephen and Helmut Korte, 'Hanna Schygulla: Der Star des Neuen Deutschen Films', in *Der Filmstar*, pp. 219–43.

Morin, Edgar, *The Stars: An Account of the Star-System in Motion Pictures* (New York and London: Evergreen Profile Books/John Calder, 1960).

Naremore, James, *Acting in the Cinema* (Berkeley, LA, and London: University of California Press, 1988).

Neale, Steve, 'Art Cinema as Institution', *Screen* vol. 22 no. 1, 1981, pp. 11–39.

Penkert, Sibylle, 'Die Geschichte der Piera', *Filmfaust* nos. 34–5, 1983, p. 30.

Penkert, Sibylle, 'Hanna Schygulla im Portrait: Von der Schwere und von der Leichtigkeit, ein Deutscher Weltstar zu sein', *Filmfaust* vol. 44, 1985, pp. 6–10.

Philbert, Bertrand, 'L'Histoire de Piera', *Cinematograph* no. 90, 1983, p. 19.

Phillips, Alastair and Ginette Vincendeau (eds), *Journeys of Desire: European Actors in Hollywood – A Critical Companion* (London: BFI, 2006).

Presber, Gabriele, 'Hanna Schygulla', in *Die Kunst ist weiblich* (Munich: Drömer/Knaur, 1988), pp. 11–35.

Qiong Yu, Sabrina, 'Introduction', in *Jet Li: Chinese Masculinity and Transnational Film Stardom* (Edinburgh: Edinburgh University Press, 2012), pp. 1–4.

Reitz, Edgar, 'Hanna Schygulla', in *Bilder in Bewegung: Essays, Gespräche zum Kino* (Reinbek: Rowohlt, 1995), pp. 144–50.

Rentschler, Eric, 'Director and Players', in Rentschler (ed.), *West German Filmmakers: Film – Vision and Voices* (New York and London: Holmes and Meier, 1988), pp. 167–8.

reuter-christiansen, ursula, 'the abused effi briest', *Frauen und Film* no. 3, 1974, pp. 3–4.

Rohrbach, Günter, 'Das Geburtstag der Hanna Schygulla', in Schirmer (ed.), *Du ... Augen wie Sterne*, pp. 35–7.

Roud, Richard, *Straub* (London: Secker and Warburg/BFI, 1971).

Schirmer, Lothar (ed.), *Du ... Augen wie Sterne: Das Hanna Schygulla Album* (Munich: Schirmer/Mosel, 1990).

Schuhl, Jean Jacques, *Ingrid Caven: A Novel* (San Francisco: City Lights Books, 2004).

Schygulla, Hanna, 'Ein autobiographischer Text', in *Hanna Schygulla*, pp. 9–38.

Schygulla, Hanna, *Hanna Schygulla: Bilder aus Filmen von Rainer Werner Fassbinder* (Munich: Schirmer/Mosel, 1981).

Schygulla, Hanna, 'Kraft zum Widerspruch', in Schirmer (ed.), *Du … Augen wie Sterne*, pp. 67–8.

Schygulla, Hanna, 'Wie alles anfing', in Schirmer (ed.), *Du … Augen wie Sterne*, pp. 42–3.

Schygulla, Hanna, 'Zu Andrzej Wajda', in Schirmer (ed.), *Du … Augen wie Sterne*, pp. 94–6.

Schygulla, Hanna, 'Hauptrolle ist schliesslich Hauptrolle', in Lars-Olav Beier and Gerhard Midding, *Teamwork in der Traumfabrik: Werkstattgespräche* (Berlin: Henschel, 1993), pp. 182–93.

Schygulla, Hanna, *Wach auf und träume: Die Autobiographie* (Munich: Schirmer/Mosel, 2013).

Seesslen, Georg, 'Heilige Huren, Bleiche Mütter', *epd Film* no. 8, August 1991, pp. 18–25.

Segreve, Kerry and Linda Martin, 'Hanna Schygulla', in *The Continental Actress: European Film Stars of the Post War Era* (North Carolina and London: McFarland, 1990), pp. 243–50.

Shattuc, Jane, *Television, Tabloids, and Tears: Fassbinder and Popular Culture* (Minneapolis and London: University of Minnesota Press, 1995).

Shingler, Martin, *Star Studies: A Critical Guide* (London: BFI, 2012).

Sieglohr, Ulrike, 'Hildegard Knef: From Rubble Woman to Fallen Woman', in Sieglohr (ed.), *Heroines without Heroes: Reconstructing National Identities in European Cinema, 1945–51* (London and New York: Cassell, 2000), pp. 113–27.

Sievenich, Chris, 'A Trailblazer', in Lorenz (ed.), *Chaos as Usual*, pp. 227–32.

Soila, Tytti (ed.), *Stellar Encounters: Stardom in Popular European Cinema* (New Barnet, Herts.: John Libbey, 2009).

Spaich, Herbert, *Rainer Werner Fassbinder: Leben und Werk* (Weinheim: Beltz, 1992).

Strauss, Frédéric, 'Entretien avec Hanna Schygulla', *Cahiers du Cinéma* no. 515, 1997, pp. 32–3.

Tesche, Siegfried, *Die neuen Stars des deutschen Films* (Munich: Wilhelm Heyne, 1985), pp. 268–81.

Töteberg, Michael and Leo A. Lensing (eds), *The Anarchy of the Imagination: Interviews, Essays, Notes*, trans. from German by Krishna Winston (Baltimore and London: Johns Hopkins University Press, 1992).

Valentini, Ruth, 'Hanna's Metamorphosen', in Schirmer (ed.), *Du … Augen wie Sterne*, pp. 153–4.

Vincendeau, Ginette (ed.), *Encyclopedia of European Cinema* (London: BFI/Cassell, 1995).

Vincendeau, Ginette, *Stars and Stardom in French Cinema* (London and New York: Continuum, 2000).

von Moltke, Johannes, 'Camping in the Art Closet: The Politics of Camp and Nation in German Film', *New German Critique* vol. 63, Autumn 1994, pp. 77–93.

Willemen, Paul (ed.), *The Films of Amos Gitai: A Montage* (London: BFI, 1993).

FILMOGRAPHY

As actor

DER BRÄUTIGAM, DIE KOMÖDIANTIN UND DER
ZUHÄLTER/THE BRIDEGROOM, THE COMEDIENNE AND THE
PIMP (Jean-Marie Straub, France, 1968), Lucy
JAGDSZENEN AUS NIEDERBAYERN/HUNTING SCENES FROM
BAVARIA (Peter Fleischmann, West Germany, 1969), Paula
DIE REVOLTE/THE REVOLT (Reinhard Hauff, West Germany,
[TV film], 1969), Sandra V.
LIEBE IST KÄLTER ALS DER TOD/LOVE IS COLDER THAN
DEATH (R. W. Fassbinder, West Germany, 1969), Johanna
DAS KUCKUCKSEI IM GANGSTERNEST/THE CUCKOO'S EGG
IN THE GANGSTER NEST (Franz-Josef Spieker, West Germany,
1969), Maria
KATZELMACHER (R. W. Fassbinder, West Germany, 1969), Marie
BAAL (Volker Schlöndorff, West Germany, [TV film], 1969)
GÖTTER DER PEST/GODS OF THE PLAGUE (R. W. Fassbinder, West
Germany, 1970), Johanna Reiner
WARUM LÄUFT HERR R. AMOK?/WHY DOES MR R. RUN AMOK?
(R. W. Fassbinder, West Germany, 1970), schoolfriend
DAS KAFFEEHAUS/THE COFFEE HOUSE (R. W. Fassbinder, West
Germany, [TV play], 1970), Lisaura
MATHIAS KNEISSL (Reinhard Hauff, West Germany, [TV film], 1970),
Mathilde Schreck

RIO DAS MORTES (R. W. Fassbinder, West Germany, 1971), Hanna

DIE NIKLASHAUSER FAHRT/THE NIKLASHAUSEN JOURNEY
(R. W. Fassbinder, West Germany, [TV film], 1971), Johanna

WARNUNG VOR EINER HEILIGEN NUTTE/BEWARE OF A HOLY
WHORE (R. W. Fassbinder, West Germany, 1971), Hanna, actress

PIONIERE IN INGOLSTADT/PIONEERS IN INGOLSTADT
(R. W. Fassbinder, West Germany, [TV film], 1971), Berta

JAKOB VON GUNTEN (Peter Lilienthal, West Germany, [TV film], 1971),
Lisa Benjamenta

WHITY (R. W. Fassbinder, West Germany, 1971), Hanna

DER HÄNDLER DER VIER JAHRESZEITEN/THE MERCHANT OF
FOUR SEASONS (R. W. Fassbinder, West Germany, 1971), Anna Epp

DIE BITTEREN TRÄNEN DER PETRA VON KANT/THE BITTER
TEARS OF PETRA VON KANT (R. W. Fassbinder, West Germany,
1972), Karin Thimm

WILDWECHSEL/WILDGAME (R. W. Fassbinder, West Germany,
[TV film], 1972), Ärztin

ACHT STUNDEN SIND KEIN TAG/EIGHT HOURS ARE NOT A DAY
(R. W. Fassbinder, West Germany, [TV mini-series], 1972), Marion

BREMER FREIHEIT/BREMEN FREEDOM (R. W. Fassbinder, West
Germany, [TV play], 1972), Luisa Mauer

DAS HAUS AM MEER/THE HOUSE BY THE SEA (Reinhard Hauff,
West Germany, [TV film], 1973), Hanna

FONTANE EFFI BRIEST/EFFI BRIEST (R. W. Fassbinder, West
Germany, 1974), Effi Briest

DER KATZENSTEG (Peter Meincke, West Germany, [TV film], 1975),
Regine Hackelberg

FALSCHE BEWEGUNG/WRONG MOVE (Wim Wenders, West
Germany, 1975), Therese Farner

ANSICHTEN EINES CLOWNS/THE CLOWN (Vojtěch Jasný, West
Germany, 1976), Marie

INTERMEZZO FÜR FÜNF HÄNDE ('Intermezzo for Five Hands')
(Ludwig Cremer, West Germany, [TV film], 1976), Lisa Wegner

DER STUMME ('The Mute') (Gaudenz Meili, West Germany, [TV film], 1976), Martha

DIE RÜCKKEHR ('The Return'), TV episode of *Die Rückkehr des alten Herrn* (Vojtěch Jasný, West Germany, 1976)

DIE DÄMONEN ('The Demons') (Claus Peter Witt, West Germany, [TV film], 1977), Dascha

SYLVESTERNACHT – EIN DIALOG ('New Year's Eve – A Dialogue') (Douglas Sirk, West Germany, [Munich Film School short], 1978)

AUSSAGEN NACH EINER VERHAFTUNG AUF GRUND DES GESETZES GEGEN UNSITTLICHKEIT ('Charge Sheet: Indecency') (George Moorse, West Germany, [TV film], 1978), The Woman

DIE EHE DER MARIA BRAUN/THE MARRIAGE OF MARIA BRAUN (R. W. Fassbinder, West Germany, 1979), Maria Braun

DIE GROSSE FLATTER ('Legging It Big Time') (Marianne Lüdcke, West Germany, [TV mini-series], 1979), Frau Piesch

DIE DRITTE GENERATION/THE THIRD GENERATION (R. W. Fassbinder, West Germany, 1979), Susanne Gast

BERLIN ALEXANDERPLATZ (R. W. Fassbinder, West Germany, [TV mini-series], 1980), Eva

LILI MARLEEN (R. W. Fassbinder, West Germany, 1981), Willie

DIE FÄLSCHUNG/CIRCLE OF DECEIT (Volker Schlöndorff, France, 1981), Ariane Nassar

LA NUIT DE VARENNES/THE NIGHT OF VARENNES (Ettore Scola, France/Italy, 1982), Countess Sophie de la Borde

PASSION (Jean-Luc Godard, France/Switzerland, 1982), Hanna

ANTONIETA (Carlos Saura, France/Mexico/Spain, 1982), Anna

HELLER WAHN/SHEER MADNESS/FRIENDS AND HUSBANDS (Margarethe von Trotta, West Germany/France, 1983), Olga

STORIA DI PIERA/THE STORY OF PIERA (Marco Ferreri, Italy/France/West Germany, 1983), Eugenia

EINE LIEBE IN DEUTSCHLAND/A LOVE IN GERMANY (Andrzej Wajda, France/West Germany, 1983), Pauline Kropp

IL FUTORO È DONNA/THE FUTURE IS WOMAN (Marco Ferreri,
Italy/France/West Germany, 1984), Anna
PETER THE GREAT (Marvin J. Chomsky, USA, [TV mini-series], 1986),
Catherine Skevronskaya
THE DELTA FORCE/MAHATZ HA-DELTA (Menahem Golan,
USA/Israel, 1986), Ingrid
BARNUM (Lee Philips, UK/Canada, [TV movie], 1986), Jenny Lind
CASANOVA (Simon Langton, UK/USA/West Germany /Italy, [TV film],
1987), Casanova's mother
FOREVER, LULU (Amos Kollek, USA, 1987), Elaine
MISS ARIZONA (Pál Sándor, Italy/Hungary, 1988), Mitzi Rozsnyai
AMORES DIFÍCILES ('Dangerous Loves') (Jaime H. Hermosillo, Spain,
[TV film], 1988)
EL VERANO DE LA SEÑORA FORBES/THE SUMMER OF MRS
FORBES (Jaime H. Hermosillo, Mexico/Spain, [TV film], 1989),
Mrs Forbes
ABRAHAMS GOLD/ABRAHAM'S GOLD (Jörg Graser, Germany, 1990),
Barbara 'Bärbel' Hunzinger
AVENTURE DE CATHERINE C./ADVENTURE OF CATHERINE C.
(Pierre Beuchot, France, 1990), Fanny Hohenstein
DEAD AGAIN (Kenneth Branagh, USA, 1991), Inga
ME ALQUILO PARA SOÑAR/I'M AVAILABLE TO DREAM FOR YOU
(Ray Guerra, Cuba/Spain, [TV mini-series], 1992)
WARSZAWA: ANNÉE 5703/WARSAW: YEAR 5703 (Janusz Kijowski,
Germany/France/Poland, 1992), Stephania
GOLEM – L'ESPRIT DE L'EXIL/GOLEM – THE SPIRIT OF EXILE
(Amos Gitai, France/Italy/Germany/Netherlands, 1992), L'Esprit de l'Exil
MADAM BÄURIN (Franz X. Bogner, Germany, 1993), Aunt Agathe
MONOLOGUES (unknown, France, [TV series short], 1993), The Widow
GOLEM – LE JARDIN PÉTRIFIÉ/GOLEM – THE PETRIFIED
GARDEN (Amos Gitai, France/Germany/Russia/Israel, 1993), Michelle
MAVI SÜRGÜN/THE BLUE EXILE (Erden Kiral, Germany/Turkey/
Greece, 1993), The Actress

AUX PETITS BONHEURS ('Here's to Life's Little Treasures') (Michel Deville, France, 1994), Lena

HEY STRANGER (Peter Woditsch, Belgium/France/Germany, 1994), Tania

LE BEL HORIZON ('The Beautiful Horizon') (Charles L. Bitsch, France, [TV film], 1994), Michèle

LES CENT ET UNE NUITS DE SIMON CINÉMA/ONE HUNDRED AND ONE NIGHTS (Agnès Varda, France/UK, 1995), Le seconde ex-épouse de M. Cinéma

ASSOCIATIONS DE BIENFAITEURS ('Associations of Benefactors') (unknown, France, [TV mini-series], 1995), Janet P. Sanders

PAKTEN/WAITING FOR SUNSET (Leidulv Risan, Norway, 1995), Ewa Loehwe

MILIM/METAMORPHOSIS OF A MELODY (Amos Gitai, France/UK, 1996), Spirit of Exile

LEA (Ivan Fíla, Czech Republic/Germany/France, 1996), Wanda

ANGELO NERO (Roberto Rocco, Italy, [TV film], 1998), Eloide Prinzivalle

LA NIÑA DE TUS OJOS/THE GIRL OF YOUR DREAMS (Fernando Trueba, Spain, 1998), Magda Goebbels

BLACK OUT P.S. RED OUT (Menelaos Karamaghiolis, Greece/France/Portugal, 1998), Martha

WERCKMEISTER HARMONIES (Béla Tarr, Hungary/Italy/Germany/France, 2000), Tünde Eszter

ABSOLITUDE (Hiner Saleem, France, [TV film], 2001), Suzanne

PROMISED LAND (Amos Gitai, USA/United Arab Emirates, 2004), Hanna

DIE BLAUE GRENZE/THE BLUE BORDER (Till Franzen, Germany, 2005), Frau Marx

FRIDAY OR ANOTHER DAY (Yvan Le Moine, Belgium/Czech Republic/France/Italy/Slovenia, 2005), La dame patronesse de l'équipage

WINTERREISE/WINTER JOURNEY (Hans Steinbichler, Germany, 2006), Martha 'Mucky' Brenninger

DAS UNREINE MAL ('The Impure Mark') (Thomas Freundner, Germany, [TV film], 2006), Gerda Albrecht

AUF DER ANDEREN SEITE/THE EDGE OF HEAVEN (Fatih Akin,
  Germany/Turkey/Italy, 2007), Susanne Staub
TOD IM WALD: STOLBERG ('Death in the Forest: Stolberg') (unknown,
  Germany, [TV series], 2008), Marita Dennett
CLARA, UNE PASSION FRANÇAISE ('Clara, a French Passion')
  (Sébastien Grall, France, [TV film], 2009), Clara
FAUST (Aleksandr Sokurov, Russia, 2011), moneylender's wife
PANDEMIA (Lucio Fiorentino, Italy, 2012)
AVANTI (Emmanuelle Antille, Switzerland/Belgium, 2012), Suzanne
THE QUIET ROAR (Henrik Hellström, Sweden, 2014), Eva
OPHELIA (Sergei Rostropovich, Germany, [short – post-production],
  2014), Vera

Hanna Schygulla's own productions

Ein Traumprotokoll, actor/director/producer/camera/sound, experimental
  short, 5 min., Germany (1976/2005)
Hanna Hannah, actor/director/script/producer, experimental short, 7 min.,
  Germany (2006/7)
Alicia Bustamante, director/script/producer/camera/editor/sound,
  documentary, 93 min., France/Cuba (2009)
Moi et mon double, director/script/producer, experimental short, 12 min.,
  France/Italy (2009)

Main acting awards

Schwabinger Art Prize (1970)
German Filmband in Gold (1970) for Ensemble Acting in *Love Is Colder than
  Death*, *Katzelmacher* and *Gods of the Plague*
German Filmband in Gold (1971) for Best Performance by an Actress in a
  Leading Role in *Whity* and *Mathias Kneissl*

German Filmband in Gold (1975) for Best Performance by an Ensemble in
  Wrong Move
Silver Bear, Berlin International Film Festival (1979) for Best Actress in *The
  Marriage of Maria Braun*
German Filmband in Gold (1979) for Best Performance by an Actress in a
  Leading Role in *The Marriage of Maria Braun*
David di Donatello (1980) for her performance in *The Marriage of Maria Braun*
Bambi for 'Woman of the Year', Germany (1981 and 1984)
Best Actress, Cannes International Film Festival (1983) in *The Story of Piera*
Special David di Donatello (1983) (for her contribution to European Cinema)
Verdienstkreuz/First Class Order of Merit of the Bundesrepublik
  Deutschland (1987)
Golden Camera (1987) for Best German Actress in the mini-series *Peter
  the Great*
European Acting Prize at the Braunschweig International Film Festival (2007)
Best Actress, RiverRun International Film Festival (2008) in *The Edge of Heaven*
National Society Film Critics Award (2009) for Best Supporting Actress in
  The Edge of Heaven
Honorary Golden Bear, Berlin International Film Festival (2010)
Star at the Boulevard of the Stars (2010)
Bavarian Order of Merit (2011)

For a complete list of awards, go to the IMDb website. Available at:
http://www.imdb.com/name/nm0778016/awards

INDEX

Notes: Page numbers in **bold** indicate detailed analysis. Those in *italic* refer to illustrations. Films are indexed under their English titles, with cross-references from the original title where necessary. *n* = endnote.

List of illustrations

While considerable effort has been made to correctly identify the copyright holders, this has not been possible in all cases. We apologise for any apparent negligence and any omissions or corrections brought to our attention will be remedied in any future editions.

Lili Marleen, Rozy-Film/CIP Filmproduktion/Rialto Film Preben Philipsen/Bayerische Rundfunk; *Katzelmacher*, antiteater-X-Film; *Love is Colder than Death*, antiteater-X-Film; *Effi Briest*, Tango-Film; *Gods of the Plague*, antiteater; *Wrong Move*, © Solaris Film/© Westdeutscher Rundfunk; *The Clown*, Heinz Angermeyer/MFG/Filmaufbau; *The Marriage of Maria Braun*, Albatros-Filmproduktion/Trio-Film/Westdeutscher Rundfunk; *Berlin Alexanderplatz*, Bavaria Film/Westdeutscher Rundfunk/Radiotelevisione Italiana; *The Story of Piera*, Faso Film; *A Love in Germany*, CCC Filmkunst/Gaumont/TF1 Films Production/Stand'Art; *Vanity Fair*, January 1984, photo: Irving Penn/Time Magazine; *The Edge of Heaven*, © Corazón International.

www.ingramcontent.com/pod-product-compliance
Ingram Content Group UK Ltd.
Pitfield, Milton Keynes, MK11 3LW, UK
UKHW020720280225
455688UK00012B/436